Individual Differences in Language Development

Sage Series on Individual Differences and Development

Robert Plomin, *Series Editor*

The purpose of the Sage Series on Individual Differences and Development is to provide a forum for a new wave of research that focuses on individual differences in behavioral development. A powerful theory of development must be able to explain individual differences, rather than just average developmental trends, if for no other reason than that large differences among individuals exist for all aspects of development. Variance—the very standard deviation—represents a major part of the phenomenon to be explained. There are three other reasons for studying individual differences in development: First, developmental issues of greatest relevance to society are issues of individual differences. Second, descriptions and explanations of normative aspects of development bear no necessary relationship to those of individual differences in development. Third, questions concerning the processes underlying individual differences in development are more easily answered than questions concerning the origins of normative aspects of development.

Editorial Board

Books in This Series

Individual Differences in Language Development

Cecilia M. Shore

Individual Differences and Development Series

VOLUME 7

P
118.6
.S48
1995
West

SAGE Publications

International Educational and Professional Publisher

Thousand Oaks   London   New Delhi

For information address:

SAGE Publications, Inc.
2455 Teller Road
Thousand Oaks, California 91320

SAGE Publications Ltd.
6 Bonhill Street
London EC2A 4PU
United Kingdom

SAGE Publications India Pvt. Ltd.
M-32 Market
Greater Kailash I
New Delhi 110048 India

Printed in the United States of America

Library of Congress Cataloging-in-Publication Data

Shore, Cecilia, M.
    Individual differences in language development/Cecilia M. Shore.
        p. cm.—(Sage series on individual differences and
    development: vol. 7)
    Includes bibliographical references and index.
    ISBN 0-8039-4879-4.— ISBN 0-8039-4880-8 (pb)
    1. Language acquisition. 2. Individual differences. I. Title.
    II. Series.
    P118.6.S48   1995   94-36207
    401'.9—dc20

95 96 97 98 10 9 8 7 6 5 4 3 2 1

Sage Production Editor: Diane S. Foster

Contents

Series Editor's Preface

One of the most striking characteristics of the human species is its natural use of language. The bursting out of language during the second year of life is also one of the most dramatic aspects of infant development, tempting us to think about ontogeny recapitulating phylogeny. These species-wide aspects of language rightfully have grabbed the spotlight for centuries, leaving in the shadows an important fact: Human infants and toddlers differ widely in the rate, style, and outcome of their language development. When we zoom in from a species-wide perspective to focus on individual children, these differences among children pop out like a figure-ground illusion. These individual differences represent an important challenge for theory and research on language because work on species-wide themes may not apply to individual variations on these themes. Although questions about individual differences might also be more important societally, especially as they shade into the abnormalities of language delays and disabilities, I also believe that once we go beyond description toward explanation, questions about individual differences in development are more tractable empirically.

For these reasons, I am especially pleased to welcome Cecilia Shore's book into the **Sage Series on Individual Differences and**

Development. Through the book's several revisions, I have been impressed with Dr. Shore's scholarliness and seriousness in grappling with this burgeoning field of research. Getting on top of this mountain of data has allowed her to show us where the field is, where it is going, and most importantly, where it ought to go—including glimpses of such distant horizons as ecological, chaos, and connectionist theories.

ROBERT PLOMIN

Preface

I'd like to thank many people who have contributed to this work either directly or indirectly, especially Marjorie Suchocki, who taught me the word "epistemology," and Elizabeth Bates, who expanded it to "genetic epistemology" and to whom I am forever indebted for her mentorship, for my intellectual life in general, and for this book in particular, and Inge Bretherton for her contributions to my understanding of infant social development.

I am grateful to Patricia Bauer, Wallace Dixon, Jr., Ling-yi Zhou, and Jim Bodle for their collaboration in some of the research described here and for their critical thinking and love of learning. Ling-yi and Jim, as well as Stacy Siebert, Blossom Richter, Betsy Davis, Christy Leak, and Shana Turner, have given me the benefit of their comments on previous drafts, and the manuscript is much improved because of them. Stacy, Blossom, Betsy, Christy, and Shana also gave me much-needed library and clerical assistance.

Thanks are also due John Bloom, Allan Pantle, Len Mark, and Marv Dainoff for discussions of "chaos theory" and connectionism.

I am very grateful to Robert Plomin, the series editor, and to C. Deborah Laughton of Sage. Their thoughtful suggestions, patience, and support have been unfailing. Thanks are given to two anonymous reviewers and to Lois Bloom for their intelligent reading and helpful comments.

Finally, my thanks go to Margaret Wright for stress-reducing "power walks," to my family for their belief in me, and especially to my husband and son, Andy and Jesse Garrison, for their support and understanding of the many evenings and weekends that "Mom has got to go work on the book."

1

Introduction:
The Importance
of Differences in
Language Development

In most textbook accounts, language development is described as proceeding from first words near the first birthday, to brief phrases about 6 months later, and then to more elaborated sentences in the third year, with the whole process of basic linguistic development complete by the age of 5 or so.[1] The premise of this book is that this sequence, in which words are being arranged into more and more elaborate sentences, like building blocks into towers, applies only to some children. Others seem to proceed in almost the opposite fashion—beginning with complex phrases that they then unpack or pull apart like pop beads. In other words, all children do not learn language in the same way. The differences among them are not simply a result of some proceeding faster along a common pathway—it appears that children can take alternate routes.

In this book, we focus on the differences between these approaches and on some of the factors that are related to children's pathways into language. This work focuses on language development from approximately 1 to 3 years of age. Although individual differences in language are often described as though we were talking about different *types of children,* as we shall see, it is probably more accurate to think of them as different *components of language* at which children may excel.

Developmental researchers are interested in language acquisition styles because they believe that the manner in which something develops may give us clues about its underlying nature or about the mechanisms that make it possible. For example, if all children developed language in the same way, one might be tempted to say that innate factors were responsible for this capacity. (Other explanations are also possible, but innate factors spring to mind.) If, on the other hand, all children do not acquire language in the same way, the different pathways that they take into language may provide clues to alternative theories about how language develops.

At a practical level, it is important to understand that normally developing children may differ from one another in ways that go beyond "faster versus slower." If we as parents or teachers believe that all children go through the same steps in acquiring language, we might be concerned if we encounter a child whose approach is quite different. The reassurance that children can acquire language in different ways may help parents be more accepting of their children's efforts, and such acceptance may facilitate language progress (Nelson, 1973).

How Does the Study of Individual Differences Relate to Theories of Language Development?

Of course, researchers have long been documenting individual differences in language development. However, prior to the early 1970s, researchers saw differences between children's language as differences in the rate of progress along a *single* developmental pathway into language. These researchers did not interpret differences between children as *qualitatively different* routes into language because of the dominant theoretical paradigms. In the 1960s, developmental psycholinguistics was dominated by a battle between two theoretical perspectives representing the two ends of the nature-nurture controversy. Neither of these gives an important role to qualitative individual differences.

EMPIRICISM

The empiricist view (associated with behaviorism, the "nurture" side) emphasizes the role of the environment. Children learn to talk because they imitate the frequent elements in their parents' speech and are reinforced for correct utterances. Given the same to-be-learned language, the general pattern of language development would be expected also to be the same. Differences between children in terms of relative degrees of progress could be expected to exist in response to environmental forces such as reinforcement for grammatically correct speech or parental modeling of a wider vocabulary.

For example, Dorothea McCarthy's (1933) classic review of research on language development described differences in children's language development associated with gender, social class, and so forth. All of these differences, however, were described in terms of relative advancement or superiority in a single developmental progression (e.g., how many months "ahead" or "behind" one group was compared to the other) (p. 304).

NATIVISM

The introduction of Noam Chomsky's transformational grammar in 1957 and the proposal of innate factors in language development caused a revolution in the study of children's language. The nativist view proposes that children are born with a "Language Acquisition Device" consisting of information about the universal characteristics of language. Each language is structured by a set of correlated rules (e.g., "If sentence subject can be deleted, then the following rules apply to pronouns . . ."). Different languages have adopted different sets of these correlated rules, but the number of possibilities is finite. A child is thought to possess innate knowledge of these possibilities and to use language input to decide which set is actually being employed by the language being acquired (Chomsky, 1968, p. 24). In other words, children learn to talk because of a universal biological program.

Nativist theories of language generally claim that the course of language development is universal and explain that this universality is due to the maturation of a language-specific mental ability that is controlled by genetic factors common to all normal human beings (Klein, 1978, pp. 9-11). Consequently, although genetic differences can exist between individuals, in nativist theories of language development individual differences are treated as either negligible or completely secondary.

As a result, although a theoretical revolution was under way in the 1960s, one thing that did *not* change was that researchers continued to ignore the possibility of qualitative individual differences. At this time, classic case studies of grammatical development were undertaken, in which some isolated comments note differences between the children (e.g., Brown, Cazden, & Bellugi-Klima, 1969). But the major thrust of these studies was to document the universal pattern of grammatical development rather than individual differences (Ramer, 1976, p. 50).

CHALLENGES TO NATIVISM

Cracks began to appear in the universalist argument as cross-linguistic studies showed that not all children acquire important grammatical elements in exactly the same sequence (Bates, Bretherton, & Snyder, 1988, p. 5; Slobin, 1982, p. 128). But even if children acquiring different languages pursued different paths, the universalist argument would still hold for children acquiring the same language—given the same to-be-learned language, the sequence of acquisition should be the same. If, on the other hand, all children do not acquire language in the same way, we question the existence of this innate Language Acquisition Device. Although the claims of universality and innateness are separable, universality has been a chosen battleground for those wishing to challenge the Chomskian position.

Lois Bloom's (1970) book *Language Development* may have been the first to "cast some doubt on the view of language development as the same innately preprogrammed behavior for all children" (p. 227). She argued that the early grammar of the three children in her study differed—no single grammatical description would cover all of them. These differences, she concluded, were not a matter of some children progressing faster than others. Rather, they reflected each child's unique experience of coming to understand the world.

The history of research on individual differences in language development has supported Bloom's contention that differences between children represent more than variation in rate of normal development and suggests that there may be more than one pathway, perhaps several different pathways, that children follow into language. The most common distinction is between "referential" and "expressive" styles, which are easiest to describe by exaggerating the differences. The classic referential pattern is the standard textbook case—single words, often nouns, giving way to multiword combinations and eventually sentences. The expressive pattern, by contrast, appears to emphasize phrases, generally of personal-social utility (e.g., "lemme see"), from the beginning and gradually comes to recognize the separability and recombinability of the individual words.

Of course, any one child's pattern of development will likely contain elements of *both* of these stereotypes. These stereotyped composite portraits also are drawn primarily from studies with a very small number of subjects, which are less reliable than large samples in telling us what characteristics tend to go together (Hardy-Brown, 1983). It may be better to think of language styles as aspects of language at which children may excel rather than as styles for different types of children. Finally, these "referential" versus "expressive" differences may be evident only in early language acquisition, before about 3 years, although there may be later traces of children's early preferences.

Researchers who study individual differences in language development believe that these variations can tell us about the mechanisms or processes that underlie language development (Nelson, 1975, p. 479). The data on individual differences in language development have led us to question time-honored "stages" of language development, the "tools" with which children go about acquiring language, and even what the "units" of language acquisition are. The "one-word period," for example, may exist only in "referential" children—"expressive" children produce phraselike utterances from the beginning (Nelson, 1975, p. 462). When linguistic structures vary in their order of acquisition, it leads to the proposal that children use different tools to acquire language. Some children are thought to rely heavily on skills that will enable them to extract relatively small units, whereas others memorize larger chunks of the language they hear (Bates et al., 1994, p. 87). It even leads to the question of whether words are the chunks of language that children acquire and by which we should measure their progress (Peters, 1977, 1983).

FOCUS ON THE CHILD'S
INTERCHANGE WITH THE WORLD

By the time researchers began to seriously investigate individual differences in language development and to construct theories that would include the possibility of individual differences, two new types of theories of language acquisition had emerged: cognitive constructivist and social interactionist. In these approaches, development involves an active interchange between the child and his or her physical and social surroundings. Both of these believe that individual differences in language are phenomena of interest.

The cognitive constructivist approach owes a great deal to Piaget's theory of cognitive development. Language is seen as one manifestation of the symbolic function, emerging at the end of the sensorimotor period of development. Language, like symbolic play, means-ends problem solving, and object permanence, is thought to rely on the underlying capacity to re-present experience. In other words, the emergence of language should be related to cognitive advances in other domains because they rely on common components (Bates, 1979). The key element of this theoretical framework is an active, problem solving approach to language and hence the expectation that children will bring to bear many of the same tools on "cracking the code" of language that they use for other tasks. Piaget himself was not interested in individual differences, but as researchers who followed in his footsteps discovered that the transition from sensorimotor action to representational thought involved several components, the possibility of individual differences emerged (Bates, 1979).

In the social interactionist view, learning language is seen as an aspect of learning to participate and exchange meanings in a social world. Infants learn to talk at least partly because older caregivers treat them as beings who have intentions and can express them and can understand the communications of others. Older caregivers structure situations and utterances in such a way as to provide the maximum support for the child's comprehension and provide verbal "scaffolding" that enables the child to participate meaningfully even with single words (e.g., Bruner, 1983). In this theoretical framework, children are active participants in a social interaction—their abilities increase as their partners give them a "leg up" into the conversation.

Recent versions of the cognitive constructivist and social interactionist perspectives give an important role to individual differences in language. The cognitive constructivist view tends to look to individual differences in language development for information about the cognitive components of language acquisition, whereas the social interactionist perspective tends to look to individual differences in language development as evidence for the different social purposes that language serves.

THE NATURE OF THE CHILD'S CONTRIBUTION: MODULARITY

A major consequence of the shift to cognitive constructivist and social interactionist views is that the content of the nature-nurture question has changed from "Is it innate or is it learned?" to "What innate preparation must the child have in order to make sense of the information available in the environment?" (Anastasi, 1958). Even nativists recognize the importance of interaction with the environment. In fact, an important goal for nativists is to specify exactly what external input is required for the normal maturation of mental capacities (Fodor, 1985, p. 35).

The argument has shifted from "Is it innate?" to "*What* is innate?" The battle over nativism in language development has become a question of domain specificity—to what extent are the tools that a child uses to acquire language *specific* to language and, even more particularly, specific to syntax? The interactionist view, which holds that language depends on abilities shared with other cognitive domains, is generally identified with a cognitive constructivist paradigm. The modularity view, which emphasizes language as one of several self-contained mental units, is generally identified with nativism. (A more complete review of these positions is found in Bates et al., 1988; Fodor, 1983, 1985; Gardner, 1983, 1985.)[2]

In general, a module is specialized to do a specific task. Its operations should be fast and be triggered (in an involuntary way) by particular types of stimuli; for example, it is difficult NOT to comprehend a simple sentence that you hear in your native language. The work of a module is difficult to bring under conscious awareness and control; for example, you cannot describe how you tell the difference between two different speech sounds or decide to do it differently. Related to this "automatic" functioning is the idea that modules are "informationally encapsulated"; that is, they work fairly independently of other cognitive operations. Modules are thought to have a biological basis, provided by evolution. They should be associated with particular brain areas and show selective impairment or sparing in disease or injury; for example, stroke patients may show specific language deficits (Fodor, 1983, 1985; Gardner, 1983, 1985).

HOW DO INDIVIDUAL
DIFFERENCES IN LANGUAGE RELATE
TO THE QUESTION OF MENTAL MODULES?

First, because of the "biological" nature of a module, it should show a characteristic developmental pace and sequence; for example, there should be language development universals. In describing the "distinctive developmental history" of language, Gardner (1983) relates the classic story of the referential child—the single-word period (in which all the examples given are nouns), the two-word telegraphic utterance period, followed by the acquisition of various forms of sentences (pp. 79-81). As we will see, the universality of this sequence is questionable.

Second, because modules work fairly independently of other abilities, individuals can specialize in this ability to the exception of others (e.g., *idiots savants)*. Correlational analyses (according to Gardner, 1983, 1985) will show that tasks that assess the skills of a module are interrelated and are less related to tasks from other domains; for example, the individual differences in verbal measures on IQ tests tend to be more related to each other than to the nonverbal scales. Modules are "the products of specific cerebral organs and . . . account for inter- and intraspecific differences in behavior" (Gross, 1985, p. 16).

There is a problem in trying to simultaneously account for (a) why human beings' language abilities surpass those of other species and (b) why individual humans' abilities differ from one another. Factors that account for differences between species may not be the same factors that explain differences within them. This problem is put vividly by McCall (1981) in his example of accounting for individual differences in the height of redwood trees—we could discover several factors that explain why this particular tree is different from its neighbor, without understanding at all how this tree species grows to be hundreds of feet tall. We need to be cautious in our interpretations—the things that cause individual differences do not necessarily cause universals. This issue is examined more closely in Chapter 5.

For the present purposes, however, individual differences in language abilities may be important clues to whether these abilities are domain specific. Is there a universal language acquisition mechanism, a common approach to learning syntax? Do syntactic abilities develop in synchrony with other aspects of language? Does the child's approach to developing syntax mirror his or her approach to other aspects of language? Does language development have links to other aspects of cognition?

On the one hand, modularity theorists answer that the child is born with the makings of a universal, content-specific language module, but there is disagreement about what aspects of language are included in the package. Fodor (1985) talks about the language module as having to contain both a grammar and a lexicon (p. 5); however, Gardner (1983) indicates that syntax and phonology are species specific and relatively autonomous, whereas semantics and pragmatics probably rely on more general cognitive abilities (p. 80).

On the other, cognitive constructivist and social interactionist perspectives tend to assume that language development *is* linked to other aspects of cognitive and social development, and they ask questions about what different cognitive abilities may underlie the observed different approaches to language, or how social input and interaction can affect the course of language development.

Plan of the Book

To address the relationships among different aspects of language and between language and cognitive/social development, we need to first get a grasp of the nature of the differences that have been observed in children's language. Most of the time, children are described as though they fit neatly into two camps, although, of course, this is a convenient fiction. How to label these approaches is something of a problem—the labels used to describe them are tinged with hypotheses about the underlying mechanisms that give rise to these differences. I have generally used "referential" versus "expressive," following the most widely used terms. But the topic of Chapter 2 is the exploration of the ways in which children differ in their acquisition of different aspects of language and how to describe the patterns that we observe.

We may wonder whether the differences we observe in language result from the general developmental level of the infants. That is, one could argue that there really is only one way to learn language, and that when we observe differences among 20-month-olds, those are not really differences of style but simply reflect differential progress along a common pathway. This would be consistent with Fodor and Gardner's contention that language, as a module, follows a single species-typical developmental trajectory. These issues are discussed in Chapter 3.

Chapter 3 also considers the relationships among development in different aspects of language. Are there autonomous subsystems (e.g., syntax) within language? This question requires that we investigate whether the approach a child takes to syntax is related in any systematic way to his or her approach to other aspects of language (e.g., vocabulary). For example, we may inquire whether children whose early vocabularies consist largely of nouns (a salient difference in early vocabulary) have predictable approaches to early sentences.

Is language distinct from cognitive/social development? Most of the explanations for individual differences in language development assume that these differences exist because of cognitive or social factors. In Chapter 4, I examine a wide range of explanations for why children choose one route into language or another. These explanations often emphasize the different cognitive tools the child uses to "crack the code" of language, or the relative salience of different social uses of language.

An implicit theme of the historical survey made in this chapter is that we see the child in our own image. Psycholinguists have tended to describe the child as a little linguist and endow the child with the same tools and methodologies that we as scientists use to try to understand language (Bloom, 1993, p. 244). When behaviorist epistemology reigned, we tended to see the child as learning language exclusively from language he or she heard—just as linguists of the day painstakingly worked out phonemes, morphemes, and phrase structure grammars from the corpora of native informants. The more modern approaches have all been strongly influenced by the digital computer metaphor—how does the hardware have to be set up in order for the child to encode and decode information and manipulate symbol strings? The last chapter shows how the technology has changed once again and that new images and metaphors affect how we think about how children go about learning and using language. Chapter 5 describes some of these new images and explores some of the ways in which they might inform our thinking about how children go about acquiring language. I also return to the question of what individual differences in language can teach us about the mechanisms of language development.

Notes

1. "At about 1 year of age, infants produce their first recognizable words. . . . For the next several months, children talk in one-word utterances. . . . They talk most about those things that interest them—objects that move, make noise, or can be manipulated. . . . At about 18 to 24 months of age, children . . . begin to combine words into simple sentences. These utterances are called "telegraphic" because they typically include only nouns, verbs, and occasionally adjectives, omitting . . . grammatical markers. . . . Telegraphic speech is . . . a universal 'child language' that has a grammar of its own. During the preschool period . . . [a]s children produce longer utterances, they begin to add grammatical morphemes" (Shaffer, 1993, pp. 399-400).

2. Although Fodor's concept of "modules" and Gardner's "separate intelligences" differ from each other, both proponents of the idea of content-specific mental devices. (For simplicity, I use the term "module.")

2

Characterizing the Nature of the Differences

There are differences in the way that children pursue each of the major areas of language aquisition: lexical/vocabulary development, grammatical development, phonological development, and pragmatic development. To get a sense of the differences that exist among children, it might be helpful to examine two very clear cases of some of the distinctions that have been observed. It is very important to remember that, of course, not all children will show such marked stylistic tendencies.

Some "Classic" Cases

A very characteristic example of one approach is Julia, described in Bates et al. (1988). When Julia was 13 months of age, she understood nearly 100 words and said 34. Nearly 80% of Julia's first words were nouns. Julia was very cautious about adding new sounds to her repertoire and produced the same sound for many words (e.g., "bah" for ball, bottle, and baby). By 20 months of age, Julia's spoken vocabulary had expanded to 290 words, nearly 90%

of which were "content" words (e.g., nouns, verbs, adjectives, and adverbs). Her first word combinations most commonly involved noun-noun combinations (e.g., "water bottle" after throwing a boy's bottle into the pool) and noun-verb combinations (e.g., her word for "love/hug/stroke" combined with "baby"). In the ensuing months, her utterances tended to leave out the little grammatical words, so they sounded like an adult telegram (e.g., "Daddy baba kitchen Julia"—Daddy is making a bottle in the kitchen for Julia). When she did begin adding the little words to sentences, she did so quite conscientiously, which was reflected in her pronunciation; for example, in "I give kiss to lion on eyes for grandma" (at 24 months), all the separate little words were given the same clear and equal stress. When she began adding word endings, such as plural "s" and possessive "'s," she was so bent on making them rule governed that she often overgeneralized them; for example, "Daddy make Julia's cry" (perhaps by analogy to "Daddy take Julia's book") uttered at 25 months.

A clearly contrasting case is Maia, described by Adamson, Tomasello, and Benbisty (1984). It was hard to tell when Maia actually began to talk. Her words were often surrounded by jabbering in sentencelike intonation contours, and words that she used at one observation might not be in her vocabulary later. Her biographers were struck by the observation that although Maia seemed interested in making sounds, she did not appear to be interested in language as such. At 15 months, she had three clear words, "sky" (for skylight), "uh-oh" (for falling down), and "doll-doll" (for the toy). At 18 months, Maia used "mama" as a general request for adult help (rather than as a name) and "no" to resist adult intervention. She responded to all questions with "uh-huh." "Socks" and "more" briefly entered her vocabulary but soon disappeared. By 20 months, Maia's utterances showed exaggerated sentencelike intonation contour, but articulation of individual sounds was very poor. Her spoken language included "mama," "no," and "uh-huh" (used in the same all-purpose ways as before), four activity words ("out," "down," "uh-oh," and "fall-down"), and two phrases ("Here da other" and "Wanta see"). Two nouns, "dada" (for daddy) and "nana" (mostly for sister), were inconsistently applied during this period. From 20 to 25 months, her vocabulary expanded rapidly to approximately 45 words, of which less than one third were nouns. Almost half (20) of her "words" were stock phrases, such as "Lemme see," "Ready to go," and "Where ya goin'?" Most of these phrases used pronouns rather than nouns to refer to objects. By 25 months, some of her utterances were combinations of separate words, but some were stock phrases, and others were partially flexible, such as "I wanna _____." Her longest utterances at that time were "That baby go in the other cup, Daddy" and "No, that one go in that cup." Julia and Maia serve as "classic cases" that I refer to throughout the chapter to illustrate contrasting emphases in vocabulary, grammar, phonology, and pragmatics.

How Do We Characterize
These Differences?

Clearly, Julia and Maia went about learning language in strikingly different ways. But how do we describe these differences? The most common terms for differences in children's language development are referential versus expressive, nominal versus pronominal, analytic versus holistic, and risk taking versus conservative. The words that we use to describe differences in children's language development have important implications.

First, these different terms capture different aspects of how children go about learning language, what it is they learn, and how these are linked. *Analytic versus holistic* terms have to do with how children make sense of the linguistic forms in utterances that they hear and relate words/phrases to the objects and events around them. These processes have implications for the *nominal (noun) versus pronominal (pronoun)* forms that children acquire. *Referential versus expressive* terms have to do with the child's grasp of the functions of language and also may have implications for the forms the child acquires. Finally, *risk taking versus conservative* terms describe children's movement through a body of knowledge over time: "fast and loose" versus "slow and careful."

However, since researchers often suspect that *how* children learn language is related to *what* they acquire, they often use referential/expressive, nominal/pronominal, analytic/holistic, and risk taking/conservative almost interchangeably. Of these terms, the risk taking/conservative dimension is least well explored. It has primarily been used as a description for patterns of phonological development, although it crops up in other areas, such as semantic development (Horgan, 1980; Rescorla, 1984, p. 103) and acquisition of grammatical morphemes (Richards, 1990). Probably the most common label is referential versus expressive, which I use as well to be consistent with the literature. The drawback to this terminology is that it suggests that only some children who emphasize certain aspects of language are being "expressive," when language always serves to express one's state of mind (Bloom, 1993).

Second, when we use terms that are opposites (e.g., referential vs. expressive) we need to be aware of how such polar opposites affect our thinking. These polar terms tend to start us thinking in terms of a typology—"there is x type of children and y type of children." Even if we know that we are describing a continuum, it is easier to characterize the extremes as though they were distinct from one another. Once we begin thinking of two distinct types (or even in terms of a continuum with opposites), it is very tempting to place value judgments on these types (or ends)— "Which one is better?" Even though most of the researchers in this area explicitly state that their goal is not to create a dichotomy (two distinct categories) or typology, such a flavor still tends to permeate this literature. One reason is the descriptive and conceptual simplicity just mentioned. Another reason is that because of the intensive nature of data collection on language acquisition, most researchers in this area are often dealing with very small samples—case studies of individual children are not at all rare. Consequently, it is easiest to describe these data by saying something like "These two children did it one way, and these other two children did it a different way." For these reasons, even though most researchers would argue that the differences they observe are not dichotomous (e.g., Bates et al., 1988, p. 66; Goldfield, 1985-

1986, p. 121; Nelson, 1985, p. 123), most research tends to describe individual differences in terms of polarities. However, as we will see, instead of thinking of *x* and *y* categories or thinking of *x* and *y* as opposites, perhaps we should think of *x* and *y* as each being areas in which children can show strengths or weaknesses.

Third, the terms we use often suggest that the child's approach to one aspect of language (e.g., vocabulary) may be paralleled in another aspect (e.g., pragmatics). If, for example, we think of differences in children's vocabulary as reflecting an "object versus social" bias, we are also likely to look for a similar pattern (i.e., referential vs. expressive) in their pragmatic use of language. Such terms also suggest likely explanations for the differences we observe. For example, if we describe the differences in object versus social terms, one is also likely to look to patterns of parent-infant interaction for explanations of these differences.

Consequently, although conceptually we can distinguish children's approach to vocabulary, for example, from their approach to grammar, it is often difficult in practice to disentangle differences in one area of language from the differences we find in some other area. For example, many children's "first words" include phrases, such as "thank you" and "stop dat," such that the distinction between vocabulary and grammar becomes blurry. However, for the present purposes, I will try to discuss each domain of language separately. In the next chapter, I focus on showing the links across different areas of language.

Lexical/Vocabulary Development

Early differences in vocabulary are impressive. Simply in terms of sheer numbers, the median number of words produced by 12-month-old infants (according to their parents) was 6, with a range from 0 to 52. By 16 months, the median was 40, but the range was from 0 to 347! (Bates et al., 1994). Recall that Julia's vocabulary far exceeded Maia's throughout the second year.

However, Julia's vocabulary differed from Maia's not only in number but also in content. Researchers often talk as though the majority of the contents (or at least the important contents) of all children's early vocabularies were nouns and that the important functions of language are naming objects and describing the world. However, children like Maia show us that children differ not only in the size of their vocabularies but also in the types of words they tend to acquire and perhaps even in what counts as a word. After examining differences in the contents of children's spoken vocabularies, I consider differences in comprehension and in the rate of overall vocabulary development.

TYPES OF WORDS IN EARLY SPOKEN VOCABULARY

The terms "referential" and "expressive" come from Nelson's (1973, pp. 22, 24) descriptions of differences in the content of children's early vocabularies. Her study involved 18 middle-class children (longitudinally from 1 to 2.5 years) and their mothers. Mothers kept diary records of the children's vocabularies, and the dyads were observed monthly in the home for hour-long visits, during which the children's comprehension, imitation, and categorization were assessed. At age 2, an hour-long free play sample (with family members as play partners) was also collected. Nelson divided the children into two groups. Referential children were defined as those who had over 50% of their first 50 words in object names (e.g., "sock," "banana"). By contrast, the children labeled expressive had a large proportion of their first 50 words in personal-social routines and formulas (e.g., "Don't do dat," "Stop it").

Relative emphasis on nouns is often considered to be stylistically important (Horgan, 1980; Snyder, Bates, & Bretherton, 1981).[1] This difference can be impressive in the 10- to 50-word range—children's vocabularies may consist of 0% to 75% common nouns (Bates et al., 1994). Preference for referential vocabulary is also consistent over time, from the infant's 25-word point to 50-word vocabulary (Pine & Lieven, 1990). Mothers' reports may tend to overestimate the number of nouns in infants' vocabularies (Pine, 1992), so that only relatively few children would actually reach the 50% nouns cutoff point in their spoken vocabularies (Bloom, 1993, pp. 195-196). Nonetheless, children do vary in their spontaneous reliance on nouns in conversation (Hampson, 1988).

Personal-social words are often considered the trademark of the "expressive" vocabulary, but some authors argue that "frozen phrases" should be recognized instead. Maia's stock phrases, such as "Lemme see," would be examples, as well as "Look at that," "Oopsadaisy," and "What's that?" (Peters, 1977). The case for the developmental and stylistic significance of frozen phrases is that with development both frozen phrases and common nouns increase from the 50-viewpoint to the 100-viewpoint word. However, they are *negatively* related to one another at both the 50-word point and the 100-word point. The negative relationship between these indicates that they are opposing tendencies in early vocabulary development. In contrast, the proportions of interactive (personal-social) words actually decreased over time, and although interactive words were negatively related to common nouns, that relationship disappeared after the first 50 words. Both of these suggest a less important developmental role for personal-social words (Lieven, Pine, & Barnes, 1992, p. 303).

Another source of individual differences in early vocabulary is the *order* in which different children acquire different types of words. Bloom and her colleagues distinguished between "substantive" words (common and proper nouns) and "relational" words (action/event/relation words, such as "allgone," "hug"). They found some children who began with substantive words and proceeded to add relational words, some who did the opposite, and yet others who showed a balanced pattern from the beginning (Bloom, 1993).

PARALLELS IN CONTENT BETWEEN COMPREHENSION AND PRODUCTION

I have described ways in which children's early productive (spoken) vocabularies may differ. Is the referential versus expressive nature of early production matched by similar comprehension? Julia, for example, both said and *understood* primarily nouns at 13 months. For understandable reasons, less is known about qualitative differences in children's early comprehension than about their production. One thing we do know is that there is often a discrepancy between the amount that children comprehend versus what they produce. For example, in a survey study of 95 youngsters, aged 12 to 16 months, some children understood nearly 250 words but produced fewer than 10 (Bates, Thal, Whitesell, Fenson, & Oakes, 1989). High early comprehension is sometimes associated with "referential" style (Bates et al., 1988; Rescorla, 1984). Although children in the survey sometimes had large gaps in size between comprehension and production, nominal and nonnominal words in comprehension and production were all correlated with one another (Bates et al., 1989).

As one would expect, consistent with the "object oriented" nature of their early productive vocabularies, referential children often showed higher comprehension of object words at 17 or 20 months than did expressive speakers (Nelson, 1973, p. 45; Snyder et al., 1981). Referential children also used words for objects in a context-flexible way (e.g., "doggie" was used not just for the family dog but for different dogs in a variety of situations), suggesting a clearer grasp of word meaning (Snyder et al., 1981). The converse also appears to be the case—children who were early comprehenders had more nouns in their productive vocabularies than did the later comprehenders (Rescorla, 1984).[2, 3]

Do children who have a large number of nouns also distinguish more different categories of *objects*? It could be that children with fewer nouns in their vocabularies might distinguish between categories *nonlinguistically* but prefer to use language for other purposes and so do not make a *linguistic* distinction between similar categories—they can tell the objects apart but do not bother to learn the different words. Children's sorting of objects is often used as a nonverbal measure of categorization. In one such study, children, aged 19 to 23 months, who sorted the objects had a significantly higher proportion of referential (two nouns) utterances in their multiword speech (according to parental interview) than did the nonsorters. These results suggest that referential language is related to more differentiated category knowledge at a nonlinguistic level (Shore, Dixon, & Bauer, in press).

DIFFERENCES IN RATE OF
ACQUISITION OF OVERALL VOCABULARY

Do referential-nominal children have an advantage in overall vocabulary acquisition? One might think so, since nouns are "open class" words. Open-class words (also called content words) are essentially limitless in number (e.g., nouns, adjectives, verbs, adverbs). By contrast, there are a definite number of closed-class words (also called function words) in a language. Children who are interested in nouns might "strike it rich" in terms of the sheer number of available words to acquire.

Several investigators suggest that children whose early vocabularies focus on nouns tend to outstrip others in rate of overall vocabulary acquisition (Nelson, 1973, p. 39, 40; Snyder et al., 1981). Julia is clearly such a case. However, considerable recent evidence exists that referentiality may not be associated with overall vocabulary precocity (Bates et al., 1994; Pine & Lieven, 1990). This issue is discussed further in the next chapter.

SUMMARY AND IMPLICATIONS

I have described differences in the content of children's early productive vocabularies, the rate of their vocabulary acquisition, and the patterns in their comprehension. In general, noun-to-total-word ratio appears to distinguish among children relatively early (Snyder et al., 1981). A tendency to rely on nouns in production tends to be paralleled in comprehension, although the sheer amount of comprehension relative to production may be very discrepant. Referentiality tends to be associated with context flexibility of words. Currently, the relationship between referential style and overall vocabulary development is somewhat controversial.

Individual differences in the contents of early vocabulary lead us to question some basic assumptions. Some researchers have suggested that children come to understand grammatical categories such as nouns by first acquiring the semantic concept of object names, so that children "pull themselves up by their bootstraps" into syntax (e.g., Pinker, 1984). Object naming plays an important role in this bootstrapping hypothesis, and some authors have suggested that infants are predisposed to believe that words are the names of whole objects (as opposed to object *parts*, for example) (Markman, 1989). However, in contradiction to the "whole object bias," some children do not have a high proportion of object names among their first words. Furthermore, if grammatical development depends on learning many object names in order to form a noun grammatical class, one would expect expressive children to be delayed in grammatical development—which does not appear to be the case (Nelson, Hampson, & Shaw, 1993).

The observation that many children make substantial use of formulas among their first "words" causes some problems, as it blurs the distinction between vocabulary and syntax (which some theorists, such as Chomsky, wish to keep separate) and calls into question the standard story that language development proceeds from one word to two words to sentences. These issues are discussed next.

Early Grammatical Development

The grammatical/syntactic system includes both word order rules and grammatical morphemes that specify the relations of the words to each other. Observers have found a number of differences in children's early multiword combinations and sentences. Some of these have to do with how grammatical relations are expressed (with nouns or pronouns); others have to do with the way in which words are combined (variable/analyzed vs. fixed/formulaic).

An analogy that might be useful in thinking about differences in early grammar is using a pocket dictionary in a foreign country. One method is to go through the dictionary and compose an utterance made of the relevant content words. You'll butcher the grammar (word order may be wrong, verb and noun endings will be missing), but you'll at least know what you said, and a sympathetic listener may be able to figure it out from the high-information content words. The other strategy is to flip to the back of the book to the "tourist phrases" and read off an utterance that suits your purposes. You'll sound more like other people, you'll get the word order and word endings right, but you won't know what the parts of the utterance mean or how to recombine those words into a new utterance.

Children like Julia, who lean heavily on the "piece together content words" strategy, would be likely to use more nominal forms (since nouns are content words). They would produce relatively few formulaic expressions or "dummy words" that are empty of apparent meaning. Their grammar would be described as "telegraphic"—meaning that they leave out the same words an adult would leave out when composing a telegram and would be reasonably consistent in their use of word order (e.g., actor tending to precede action). Consistent with their use of telegraphic grammar, they would use relatively few grammatical inflections (e.g., plural "s," past tense "-ed").

By contrast, children like Maia, who rely heavily on the "tourist phrases" strategy, would tend to have a larger number of pronominal forms. Many of their early sentences would be formulaic, and "dummy words" would often be used to "fill out" the sound of a sentence. Their grammar would be described as "pivot open" or "frame slot"—meaning that a small number of anchoring words are combined with variable elements (e.g., "do it," "get it," "fix it"). Other than these frames, their utterances would not show remarkable word order consistency. Partly because of the high reliance on frozen phrases, they would have a relatively high use of grammatical inflections.

These portraits are overdrawn to distinguish these different approaches. I now go back and examine the evidence for individual differences in each of these aspects of grammar. Later, I return to the question of how well these "hold together" in two composite portraits by looking at the relations among different multiword forms and examine some implications of differences in children's approaches to grammar.

USE OF NOMINAL VERSUS PRONOMINAL FORMS

Nominal versus pronominal approaches to early grammar were first described by Bloom (1970). Bloom, Lightbown, and Hood (1975) followed four children from their earliest multiword utterances to MLU (mean length of utterance) 2.5, a time span covering ages 19 to 26 months. The children were visited in the home at either 3- or 6-week intervals, and their language was recorded as well as notes about the relevant nonlinguistic context. Bloom et al. were interested in the words that children used to express a number of basic meanings, such as agent (the "do-er"), action, affected object, and place. Prior to MLU 2.0, the two boys tended to use pronominal terms to encode agent or mover ("I"), affected object ("this"), and place ("here"). The two girls, however, used nominal terms for these meanings, such as "Mommy" as agent, "book" as affected object, and "table" as place (pp. 18-19). A salient example is children's use of names versus personal pronouns. Pronominal speakers typically do not refer to themselves by name, whereas nominal speakers may resist using pronouns and persist in using their names (Bloom, 1970; Huxley, 1970).

Nelson (1975) found that children's reliance on nominal versus pronominal forms in their sentences is related to earlier differences in their vocabularies. Children (from the 1973 study) whose early vocabularies were referential tended to use nouns in early multiword utterances (when followed up at 24 and 30 months of age). Children whose early vocabularies were "expressive" tended to use pronouns in their early multiword utterances. Like Bloom et al., Nelson looked to see whether children used nouns or pronouns to express basic meaning categories. In general, although the two groups expressed the *same* basic meaning categories, expressive speakers used pronouns at least 70% of the time to express these meanings, whereas referential speakers did so less than 60% of the time. These differences in relative use of nouns versus pronouns are clear in Julia's and Maia's respective utterances: "I give kiss to lion on eyes for grandma" versus "No, that one go in that cup."

The advantages of a nominal strategy may be clear, but why might children use a pronominal strategy? Nelson (1975) argues that because young children tend to talk about the here and now, these generic terms (e.g., "that") are generally interpretable in context. Perhaps more important, these general terms simplify the language learning task in some ways. They make it possible for children to learn the basic forms of sentences without worrying about the specific words to be used. Relationships between things can be described without having to search for the particular names of those things (pp. 476-477). The disadvantage of relying on generic words comes in talking about objects that are not present (Nelson, 1975, p. 478; Rescorla, 1984, p. 109).

FORMULAIC EXPRESSIONS

Observers are often struck by young children's ability to incorporate whole segments of conversation. Parents will resonate to Bloom's (1970) description of Eric's remarkable ability to recite the text of his favorite books, even turning the pages at the appropriate points. Some children, like Maia, seem to have, among their earliest "words," frozen, unanalyzed phrases treated as a unit. Until recently, relatively little theoretical attention has been paid to children's early production of formulaic utterances. In this section, I first present evidence that these unanalyzed phrases are common enough to warrant investigation as a route into grammar and then some suggestions as to how frozen phrases could lead into productive use of grammar. ("Productive" in grammar means that the words are separate units that can be recombined to make novel sentences.)

Several case studies, such as Maia's, as well as group studies (e.g., Nelson, 1973, p. 39) give evidence of children having two types of language—analytic and gestalt—and that the gestalts often include formulaic utterances such as "look at that," "oopsadaisy," "what's that?", "thank you," "hey you guys," "let's go," "bless you," and "lemme see" (Goldfield, 1985-1986; Peters, 1977). I/you reversals, such as "sit my knee" and "I carry you," provide a strong hint that these sequences are "unopened packages" from adult utterances (Clark, 1974, p. 3). When children use many formulaic utterances, their approach is often characterized as "holistic" because they appear to pick up phrases as a whole unit. Other children, who seem to treat words more like building blocks to be put together into sentences, are described as employing an "analytic" strategy. Comparable analytic versus holistic approaches have been observed in children learning English as a second language or learning other languages, such as Danish (Fillmore, 1979; Plunkett, 1985).

Eventually, however, formulaic utterances need to be analyzed into words that can be productively recombined into new utterances. Clark (1974) argues that the few productive rules her subject used frequently began as formulaic "invariable routines." Some interesting accounts of this differentiation exist. One example shows the progression for "How do you do dese?" from formulaic to productive use of the individual question word "how" (Fillmore, 1979). Another example of "fissioning" a chunk into smaller units: "I don' wan' she to talk to me" breaks into other forms, such as "don' wan'" and "don' talk to me" (from Iwamura, cited in Peters, 1983). Children can also create new utterances by sticking together two unanalyzed chunks, resulting in, say, "That's mine jam" and "Where's Adam upstairs?" (Peters, 1983, pp. 72-78). Such juxtapositions can result in analysis. One such "magic moment" was recorded when a child produced first "You want to have a bath?" (apparently from the adult utterance, "Do you want to have a bath?") and then "I want teddy have a bath." He then modified this to "I want teddy *to* have a bath" (emphasis added) (Clark, 1977, p. 356).

In sum, formulaic utterances make up a relatively large portion of some children's speech and are plausible as a starting point for analysis into productive speech. These observations have led some observers to question the traditional "language milestones" of one word, then two, and then sentences (Nelson, 1975, p. 478). The "units of language acquisition" seem to be different for different children (Peters, 1977).

DUMMY WORDS AND REDUPLICATED FORMS

Other strategies that may also help the child sound more like other speakers and provide a "leg up" into syntax are "dummy words" and reduplicated forms. Dummy words occur when children get the overall intonation contour of the sentence correct and "fill in" around the content words with empty syllables. Probably the most famous of these was produced by Lois Bloom's daughter, Allison, whose early sentences included a syllable, "wida," which did not seem to have a clear referent (Bloom, 1973). Similar dummy words or "filler syllables" (e.g., "uh-uh down") have been observed in other expressive speakers (Nelson, 1973, p. 111; Peters, 1977, p. 564).

Reduplicated forms appear when the child repeats words or phrases within an utterance. Some such utterances seem to "build up" to the next one—for example, "Baby Ivan have a bath, let's go see *baby Ivan have a bath.*" Another type involves repeating the whole previous utterance when asked by an adult to expand or clarify—for example, "Mummy you go." "Where?" "Mummy you go swings" (Clark, 1974, p. 2).

Dummy words and reduplicated forms may be presyntactic forms that are used by some children to smooth the transition into grammar. They have been observed to be used by children who are developing syntax more slowly. Rapid syntactic developers tended not to use these forms to any great extent and tended to put them aside when true syntax emerged. Consequently, these forms "appear to be a way of easing into syntax" (Ramer, 1976, p. 55) because they allow the child to combine elements without having to worry about the meanings of words, or word order, or grammatical elements showing the relationships among things.

PIVOT-OPEN VERSUS TELEGRAPHIC GRAMMAR

Pivot-open grammar means that early word combinations tend to have a high frequency function word such as "no" or "allgone" plus a variable content word such as "shoe" or "cookie"— for example, "allgone shoe," "allgone cookie." This is in contrast to telegraphic utterances, which tend to have content words, often nouns, but no function words—for example, "Mikey milk," "daddy truck." Maia's partly frozen, partly flexible utterances such as "I wanna _____" would be considered "pivot-open" in structure, whereas Julia's "Daddy bottle kitchen Julia" would be described as extremely telegraphic.

In the 1960s, when researchers first started writing grammars of child language with the goal of describing the operation of a universal Language Acquisition Device, some studies emphasized the telegraphic nature of early grammar while others emphasized its pivot-open structure. Lois Bloom (1970) may have been the first to point out this contradiction, raising questions about the universality of early grammar (p. 140). In her study, the grammar of one subject, Eric, would be described as having a pivot-open structure. The other two children, Kathryn and Gia, had produced utterances of the more telegraphic type. Eric developed verb-object combinations first, while the two girls expressed subject-verb, subject-object, and verb-object relations. Bloom argues that Eric's language was not simply more immature because his utterances were, on average, longer (pp. 131-133). Rather, she thinks that there may not be one universal pattern of children's language development.

Bloom suggests that cognitive development influences whether children lean toward a pivot-open grammar or a telegraphic one. She says that pivot-open structures may reflect the child's recognition of the functional-relational words (e.g., "more," "allgone") that apply to particular situations so that he or she can later acquire other words relevant to those situations (e.g., "cookie") and use these in combinations. That is, this general formula (e.g., "more ____") is useful at lunchtime and different food words can be used in the slot. In these context-dependent combinations, the *relationship* between the words depends on the meaning of one of them: The link between "more" and "cookie" in "more cookie" depends on the meaning of "more" (Bloom, 1973, p. 116).

Telegraphic-type utterances, on the other hand, emphasize a different recognition, namely, one of linguistic categories that are independent of the meanings of particular words. In a sentence expressing a possessive relationship (e.g., "mommy sock"), the relationship between the words does not depend on the meaning of either individual word. Furthermore, different words can enter into the same possessive relationship with one another.

Individual differences in children's reliance on pivot-open versus telegraphic speech also appeared in Braine's (1976) study of early word combinations. These alternative strategies (pivot-open structures vs. linguistic categories) are not mutually exclusive. Both appear to be used by different children to different extents (Bloom, 1973, p. 123; Bloom et al., 1975). Children can even change their pattern of reliance on these strategies, as did Bloom's daughter Allison, perhaps (as Bloom suggests) because of increases in vocabulary and understanding of events and relationships.

CONSISTENCY IN THE USE
OF WORD ORDERING RULES

Not only do children evidently differ in the rules they use for combining words, but they also apparently differ in the extent to which they even consistently employ word order. For example, Braine (1976) noted variability in ordering principles used by children (p. 92). This is contrary to Brown et al. (1969), who indicated that the children they studied rarely produced word order errors.

Generally, it would be consistent with the stereotype of referential-analytic speakers to be more consistent about word order—except (of course) for the formulaic phrases at which expressive-holistic children are said to excel (Horgan, 1980, p. 7). However, this may be a situation in which the child's referential-analytic versus expressive-holistic tendencies are independent of his or her risk taking versus conservative tendencies. Some expressive-style children seem to be inconsistent (or error prone) in terms of word order rules (Horgan, 1980, p. 11; Vihman & Carpenter, cited in Bates et al., 1988, p. 48). For example, Lieven (1978) says that the 25-month-old expressive child in her study would combine seemingly randomly the small stock of words she had, producing utterances like "there Sebastian" and "Sebastian there." However, other children, who had many dummy forms and reduplicated constructions (usually thought of as expressive characteristics) showed a great deal of consistency in word order rules (Ramer, 1976).

Not only do expressive tendencies apparently occur with both consistent and inconsistent word orderings, but referential tendencies are not completely associated with perfectly consistent word orders (Ramer, 1976). For example, Bloom (1970) says that her subject Gia (a telegraphic speaker) did produce variations of word order (e.g., both "read book" and "book read") (p. 167). The risk taking versus conservative dimension may be more closely associated with word order variability than is the referential-analytic versus expressive-holistic.

INFLECTIONS AND GRAMMATICAL MORPHOLOGY

I have distinguished between nominal versus pronominal styles and pivot-open versus telegraphic grammars. A related observation is that some children (like Julia) emphasize open-class content words, whereas others (like Maia) focus on closed-class function words and grammatical morphemes, for example articles, prepositions, and suffixes such as "-ing" (e.g., contrast Sarah and Eve, in Brown et al., 1969). Some researchers have used statistical techniques to see which language variables (from maternal interviews at 20 months) were most closely correlated with one another. They found a "nominal/referential" cluster of variables, such as noun-noun combinations, that was separate from a "grammatical morpheme" cluster of variables, such as the tendency to use inflections, articles, prepositions, and auxiliary verbs in multiword utterances (as well as two other clusters) (Bretherton, McNew, Snyder, & Bates, 1983; Shore, 1986).

There appear to be different ways to go about learning function words and inflections. Some children appear to seek an organized rule system that, once attained, allows rapid generalization. These children may start off with relatively little "fancy morphology" because they use relatively few unanalyzed forms. Once they find a rule, however, they may rapidly put it to work—even overgeneralizing it (e.g., "runned" for "ran" is an overregularization). For example, Julia initially used very few grammatical morphemes, and when she began using them tended to overgeneralize them. Because Mean Length of Utterance (MLU) is based on morphemes, including function words and inflections, such children may show rapid gains in productive MLU. Other children may, early on, appear to have an advantage because they use function words and inflections in unanalyzed formulas. For example, Maia's "Where ya goin?" is made of four morphemes, a large number per utterance for this age range. Because the function words and inflections are frozen in formulas, these children may also make relatively few mistakes. However, their use of stereotyped forms may make it harder for them to make rapid progress in analyzing phrases into separate morphemes and recombining them into new utterances (Richards, 1990, p. 217).

In general, the more analytic approach to acquiring function words and inflections is thought to be associated with referential style, whereas the more holistic approach is thought to be associated with expressive style. "Noun-loving" children have been observed to make rapid progress but to have more errors in pronoun and verb use or errors in morphological overregularizations (Horgan, 1980). Such overregularizations could easily result from an effort to apply linguistic rules consistently (Bates et al., 1988, p. 48). The slower children ("noun leavers") in Horgan's study showed nonsignificant tendencies to use more varied constructions and more verbs and auxiliaries ("helping" verbs). Perhaps they were delayed by "spreading themselves more thinly" than the faster group (Goldfield & Reznick, 1990; Horgan, 1981, p. 637). However, these children showed good comprehension, and 3 months later they had nearly caught up with the average MLU for their age.

SUMMARY AND IMPLICATIONS

We have seen that children may differ considerably in how they go about acquiring syntax. Children show differences in both aspects of syntax, word order rules, and grammatical morphemes. Bloom's (1970) summary of her results on pivot-open versus telegraphic grammar is also very apt here: "It appears that the results of this study would cast some doubt on the view of language development as the same innately preprogrammed behavior for all children" (p. 227).

Researchers have frequently described these differences as a distinction between a nominal-analytic approach to grammar and a more expressive-holistic strategy. One could argue that both analytic and holistic methods are useful in acquisition. The utility of analytic methods is perhaps obvious. However, a holistic method also has utility. If you listen to fluent speech in another language, you realize that words are not easily identifiable in the speech stream. Furthermore, much of everyday language is formulaic (e.g., "Excuse me," "I'm sorry") (Peters, 1983). Consequently, there is not a clear distinction between words and sentences. Beginning language users have to isolate the parts they will work with and figure out when to use those parts and how to recombine them. Consequently, most children will exhibit aspects of both formulaic and analytical use, and a balanced account of language development cannot focus exclusively on the analytical word-to-sentence progression (Nelson, 1985, p. 108; Peters, 1983).

Further support for the importance of *both* types of approaches is that languages differ along this analytic-holistic dimension. Some languages, such as Russian and Finnish, attach particles to other words to indicate relationships such as indirect object. Other languages, such as English, express these relationships by using combinations of separate words (e.g., "I gave the book *to the* boy"). Perhaps all children have the capacity for both types of systems (Bloom et al., 1975, p. 34).

If analytic and holistic approaches represent dimensions along which children can differ, one would expect to see variables representing a nominal-analytic strategy correlating with one another in a relatively large sample of children. Similarly, one would expect to see intercorrelated variables representing the expressive-pronominal approach. In a pair of studies (Dixon & Shore, 1991a, 1992), factor-analytic methods were used in relatively large samples (*Ns* = 87 and 56) of 20- to 22-month-old infants to explore the relationships among measures of linguistic form. All parents were administered a language interview based on that validated by Bretherton et al. (1983). As expected, body parts vocabulary (as a rough indicator of overall vocabulary) and multiword utterances with two nouns were strongly related to one factor. The other factor was related to multiword utterances containing pronouns only, neither nouns nor pronouns, and morphological elements, such as inflections, articles, auxiliaries, or prepositions. The results support the view that stylistic differences can be thought of as dimensions common to a large number of children (rather than as a dichotomy).

If we think of holistic-formulaic approaches as being part of the tool kit that children use to "crack the code" of language, we may be able to simplify some of our explanations for some aspects of syntactic development (Clark, 1974). For example, the child's first wh-questions are essentially the same as statements, with the addition of an initial question word or question intonation ("Where Daddy going?") (Brown, 1968). We could explain these by saying that although the child has knowledge of grammatical rules, such as reversing order of subject and verb, the child does not have the memory capacity to implement these changes in the sentence (Bellugi, 1971, p. 101). However, it is simpler to see early questions as utterances treated as unanalyzed wholes plus a question word (Clark, 1974, p. 8).[4]

Phonological Development

There are several ways in which children appear to differ in how they learn the sounds of their language. First, not all children who are learning the same language appear to acquire phonemes (individual sounds—e.g., "b" in "bat") in the same order. This is contrary to what one might have predicted if phonological development were controlled primarily by biological factors (Gardner, 1983, p. 80). Second, some children (like Julia) seem to focus on individual sounds, whereas others (like Maia) seem to emphasize the sound characteristics of the utterance as a whole. This distinction may be analogous to analytic versus holistic approaches to grammar—some children focus on words while others focus on phrases as a whole. A third distinction will also sound familiar— some children tend to be risk takers in the overall pattern of additions to the phonological system, whereas others appear to be more conservative. Finally, a related observation is that some children try to keep different words separate by acquiring new sounds to distinguish them, whereas others try to make each syllable cover the maximum amount of lexical territory. For example, Julia was cautious about adding new sounds and tried to make the ones she had stand for as many objects as possible.

SEQUENCE OF PHONOLOGICAL DEVELOPMENT

Do all children begin with a biologically programmed set of sounds, which are then modified by linguistic experience? If this were the case, several predictions might follow:

1. We would expect variability in sound production to be initially very low and then increase. However, in one study of 10 children's first 50 words, variability in how different phonemes were produced tended to *decrease* (Vihman, Ferguson, & Elbert, 1986).
2. We would also expect that the initial set of phonetic characteristics would be similar across children. This does not appear to be the case. Some sounds appeared in all children's repertoires, some sounds in only a few children's, and some in none of the children's repertoires. Some played an important role for *some* children at *some* points in time (Goad & Ingram, 1987; Vihman et al., 1986).
3. We would also expect that the initial repertoire would draw heavily from sounds that are common to a wide variety of languages. On the contrary, the list of sounds that were highly used versus not highly used did not correspond to universals across languages (Vihman et al., 1986).

Evidently, children do follow different paths in the acquisition of specific sounds. Phonology is so variable and complex that it is likely that different children will have different analyses (Ferguson, 1979, p. 199).

PROSODY VERSUS PHONEMIC
ANALYSIS AND INTELLIGIBILITY

A number of different studies distinguish between children on the basis of clarity of articulation, or an emphasis on prosody (intonation) versus phonemic analysis. In a sort of trade-off, some children show clear articulation of distinct phonemes, whereas others maintain the prosody of overall sentences but blur the details of individual sounds. Maia would be an example of the latter approach, emphasizing intonation over intelligibility.

Another such child showed a distinctive "melody" for more than half of his utterances (Dore, 1974). Many of the formulaic utterances noted above (e.g., "thank you," "uh-oh," "whassat?" and "oopsadaisy") tend to be holistically produced without pauses between words with blurry articulation but with clear intonation (Peters, 1977). Sometimes, the intonation alone, content free, seems to be the point of interest—Eric (Bloom's pivot-open subject) would play a dialogue game, taking turns making utterances with nonsense content but sentencelike intonation (Bloom, 1970, p. 236). Another expressive child produced at 18 months "a lengthy unintelligible 27-second discourse, embellished with the pauses, gesticulations, and gathering momentum of a personal narrative" (Goldfield, 1985-1986, p. 128).[5]

Do these phonological differences arise from developmental differences, or are they a matter of style? If phonological development means distinguishing clearly among different phonemes, then unintelligible children are by definition less advanced. In a longitudinal study of 10 children, unintelligible children made more *phonological* errors (e.g., simplifying consonant blends, or substituting an easier sound for a harder one) (Vihman & Greenlee, 1987).

However, there are several reasons to believe that, beyond developmental differences, a stylistic difference may exist in whether children emphasize large units of sound versus individual phonemes. First of all, we can distinguish between *phonological* errors (representing phonological development) and *prosodic* errors. These are errors affecting the whole word (e.g., rearrangement of sounds; assimilations, or producing different neighboring sounds in the same way; or deletions of sounds or syllables). Prosodic errors were not correlated with phonological error scores or with consistency of pronunciation of particular sounds. Consequently, these prosodic errors were thought to represent factors other than developmental lag (Vihman & Greenlee, 1987). Another reason to be cautious in attributing prosodic-unintelligible speech to slower development is that in at least one case the child initially possessed clear articulation but, over time, tended toward more unintelligible utterances with adultlike intonation contour (Goldfield, 1985-1986). Furthermore, "developmental lag" would not explain why context affects the probability of this type of utterance—children may engage in more long nonword vocalizations when they are alone (Vihman et al., 1986).

PHONOLOGICAL LEARNING STYLES

Children's phonological development can be characterized in terms of learning styles that by now will sound familiar—cautious systematic versus bold scattered. Some children are described as "cautious system builders" who have a clear phonological system and who acquire words that are consistent with those rules. These children work on small groups of phonetically related sounds and systematically expand them (Ferguson, 1979; Vihman et al., 1986). Other children are said to be willing to try new sounds of different types and to have a frequently changing variety of sounds in their repertoire (Ferguson, 1979; Vihman et al., 1986). One such child at 19 months had eight different pronunciations of "horsie" (Peters, 1977, p. 563). Such learning styles appear to be a reliable characteristic from 1 to 3 years of age (Vihman & Greenlee, 1987) and appear in children learning different languages, although not all children can be characterized as belonging exclusively to either of these styles.

Children's phonological strategies may affect how they make use of adult input. Children whose phonological development is rule governed may resist imitating words that do not fit, whereas other children with less rigid systems may imitate more different words and "show improvement in production as a result of direct modeling" (Goldfield & Snow, 1989, p. 307; see also Macken, 1978). Julia's mother recounts how she tried 10 times to get Julia to modify her pronunciation of "horsie" from "sheeshee" to "horsie" and how Julia reluctantly compromised with "hah-sheeshee" (Bates et al., 1988, pp. 248-249).

DIFFERENTIATING VERSUS
SIMPLIFYING APPROACHES TO
PHONOLOGICAL SYSTEM DEVELOPMENT

Some children evidently work to keep words distinct from one another and avoid homonyms. Other children may try to make the same sound pattern cover as many meanings as possible and merge adult words, thereby creating homonyms (e.g., Julia's "ba" for "ball," "baby," and "bottle") (Stoel-Gammon & Cooper, 1984; Vihman, 1981). One might think of these styles as embodying a speed-accuracy trade-off, as children who use the same sound pattern for many different meanings could be said to be rapidly expanding their vocabularies.

Do these mergers and homophones arise because of a failure to perceptually distinguish the sounds, articulation (pronunciation) difficulties, or a more central strategy? In some cases, the mergers are evidently strategic: The child began with different pronunciations of words that are phonetically similar in the adult language, but soon these words converged on a similar pronunciation (Vihman, 1981, p. 245). Other word mergers may have a perceptual basis. For example, Vihman's son first learned "throw" (accompanied by a throwing gesture) and later "water," which in Estonian sound similar. For several months he pronounced these words the same way and accompanied both with the same gesture. These "slips of the ear" may result from storing words as wholes (Vihman, 1981, p. 249).

SUMMARY AND IMPLICATIONS

Phonology, like syntax, has been claimed to be an aspect of language development that is relatively autonomous, isolated from other aspects of development, largely biologically based, and under maturational control (e.g., Gardner, 1983, p. 80). This view is questionable. If phonology were largely under maturational control, children's phonological development would show a common characteristic pattern. However, not all children learning the same language acquire phonemes in the same orderly fashion. They do not appear to begin with the same "starter set" of sounds and do not appear to add new sounds in accordance with the same pattern or timetable. Rather, they differ in terms of their overall orientation to learning the sounds of their language. Some children appear to emphasize the "tune," whereas others focus on the details of the "notes." Some add new sounds cautiously; others appear to proceed in a more diverse way.

Furthermore, phonological development does not appear to be isolated from other aspects of development. We have seen a number of ways in which the analytic versus holistic dimension or the cautious versus bold quality of phonological development could be analogous to similar approaches to grammatical development. Some authors have suggested that this parallel goes beyond analogy. Phonological risk takers, children who try a variety of consonants, may be more likely to produce gestalt or holistic utterances. Their words were more likely to have "filler syllables" to round out the utterance to sound more like a sentence than were those of more phonologically cautious children (Vihman, 1986). Phonological consistency or variability may also be associated with consistency or variability in the child's use of grammatical rules (Vihman & Carpenter, cited in Bates et al., 1988, p. 52).

Another way in which phonological development is not autonomous is that it appears to be related to vocabulary development. Children may differ in which of these (phonology or vocabulary) takes the lead. Some authors argue that the words children want to acquire determines the sounds they learn to make and that the semantic function of keeping meanings distinct drives the child to learn different sounds (Drachman, also Ingram, cited in Vihman, 1981; Ferguson & Farwell, 1975, p. 437). However, Vihman's (1981) data indicate that at least *some* children do precisely the opposite—favorite sounds or phonological similarity may have encouraged the child to incorporate this group of words into his or her productive vocabulary. Rather than learning new sounds to distinguish different words, these children may merge words, with the seeming goal of covering the maximum number of lexical items with the minimum of sound shapes. In Vihman's terms, they value efficiency over clarity. Plunkett (1993) also argues that once children solve the problem of how to segment the utterances they hear into separate words, they are ready for a rapid expansion of their vocabularies. Regardless of whether semantics or phonology leads, the sounds that children produce are linked to the words they are learning, and phonological development is not autonomous.

Pragmatic Development

Pragmatics, the social use of language, reflects the functions that language serves. Among other things, language serves informational and interpersonal functions. The informational function of language involves describing the state of the world, while the interpersonal function has to do with influencing/relating to other people. Researchers often suspect that children, early on, may tend to focus on one of these language functions more than the other. Nelson (1985), for example, emphasizes that referential versus expressive styles in vocabulary development arise from children's differing perception of the function of language. Referentially oriented children are said to perceive language as primarily informational, whereas expressive children are thought to intuit that the primary purpose of language is interpersonal. Some researchers do find differences between children in the pragmatic functions of their utterances. Others find differences in children's understanding of conversational principles. Questions arise, however, regarding the relationship between form and function—is it really the case that nominal language is particularly suited for referential functions? Questions also arise as to whether a different approach to *language* implies a different approach to the object or social *world*. These are discussed further in the chapter on explanations.

INFORMATIONAL VERSUS
INTERPERSONAL FUNCTIONS

Children evidently differ in their use of language for categorizing objects versus interacting with people (Lieven, 1978; Plunkett, 1985). For example, in a study of 2 subjects, the girl, although she produced more words, used language for fewer different purposes (e.g., labeling, requesting action, greeting, protesting). The boy used language for more different functions and more of them involved other people (e.g., requesting, answering a question). The girl's language functioned mostly to represent the world to herself, whereas the boy's was more instrumental (to accomplish something) (Dore, 1974).

ORIENTATION TO CONVERSATION/CONTEXT

Several authors indicate that referential children's utterances are more coherent and conversationally relevant (Lieven, 1978, p. 186). For example, three "early comprehender-nominal" children seemed to be more oriented to language as a medium. When spoken to, they seemed to pause, reflect, and respond. The three other children were described as "impervious to language." When spoken to, they just continued with what they had been doing (Rescorla, 1984). Maia was also described as uninterested in language as such.

DO FORM AND FUNCTION COINCIDE?

Nelson argues that the children who emphasize informational functions in their early language are referential and that those who emphasize interpersonal functions are expressive. Low MLU nominal-referential children are more likely than comparable pronominal-expressive children to use their nouns to identify referents (the things being talked about) and to use language for referential functions, whereas pronominal-expressive children used their language for more personal functions (Furrow, 1980, cited in Nelson, 1985, p. 112; Lucariello & Nelson, 1986; Nelson, 1975). The reason is that nominal forms are said to be particularly useful/frequent for referential purposes/contexts and pronominal forms particularly appropriate for interpersonal purposes/contexts (Nelson, 1985).

However, other authors have argued that there is not a strong association between form and function. First of all, nouns, pronouns, and other words can perform a variety of functions, making classification into parts of speech difficult (McCarthy, 1933, p. 293). Furthermore, the use of a given word may shift over time. Bowerman (1976) cites Ferrier's example of a child who initially used "phew!" expressively as a morning greeting (echoing her mother's expression upon encountering a distinctive smell). Later, the child used "phew" referentially as a label for diapers (whatever their state of cleanliness).

Referentiality of vocabulary does not necessarily correspond to the child's orientation to language. Though all six of Rescorla's (1984) subjects would have been technically counted as referential (based on the criterion of 50%+ nominals in the first 50 words), they differed considerably in their sensitivity to language as a means of communication. In another study of seven subjects, there was continuity from 50 to 100 words in the *functional* categories of utterances (e.g., attention, label, describe, demand, protest). However, this was *unrelated* to referentiality of vocabulary (Pine, 1992). Worse yet, there was no correlation between maternal measures of vocabulary composition at 50 words and the functional use of words in conversation (Pine, 1992).

ARE EXPRESSIVE CHILDREN MORE SOCIAL?

Although expressive children are often thought to emphasize the interpersonal functions of language, Bates et al. (1988), Bretherton et al. (1983), and Nelson (1981) dispute the notion that expressive children are more *social* than referential children. Bretherton et al. (1983) say that "mommy milk" can be just as effective a command as "I wan' dat" (p. 311). Both informational and interpersonal pragmatic functions, expressed in nominal or pronominal terms, since they both involve communicative intent, could be said to entail social motivation (Bates et al., 1988, p. 51). Ironically, in both Rescorla's (1984) and Lieven's (1978) studies, it is the expressive children, those who would be thought of as the most socially oriented in their language, who are described as "impervious to language," or conversationally inept.

SUMMARY AND IMPLICATIONS

Although language is always "expressive" in the sense that it serves to express internal states (Bloom, 1993), children do apparently differ in the degree to which they emphasize informational versus interpersonal functions of language. They also differ in the degree to which they attend to language as a medium of communication and carry on coherent discourse. It is, however, not clear how these differences relate to stylistic dimensions in other aspects of language such as vocabulary. Informational versus interpersonal pragmatic functions, such as informing or commanding, could be carried out with either a referential or an expressive vocabulary. To examine Nelson's idea that children's understanding of the functions of language drives their acquisition of language forms, more work is needed that examines the relationship between vocabulary and its use in context.

A Look Forward

We have seen a number of different characterizations of the dimensions of differences among children's early language: referential versus expressive, nominal versus pronominal, risk taking versus conservative, and analytic versus holistic. We have also seen a strong tendency to suspect that a child's strategy in one aspect of language (e.g., lexical development) is paralleled in, for example, phonological development. When there are such linkages or similarities of approach in different areas, researchers begin to speak of different "styles" of language development that can be described in these dichotomous terms. One is tempted to overlay all of these dimensions onto one another as though they really constituted different manifestations of the same underlying dimension—an "analytic" approach to language or a "risk taking" approach to language. Terms like "analytic" or "expressive" are then often used as a sort of shorthand to refer to individual differences in language and as starting points for thinking about the origins of these differences. We are tempted to use such terms to make a leap from description to explanation.

However, it can be difficult to ascertain how individual differences in performance relate to underlying mental abilities. If we want to argue that children's approach to vocabulary is related to their approach to phonology, that they represent some underlying common mental ability or proclivity, then the activities that reflect one such ability should be more closely related to each other than they are to other activities. There are other criteria also for determining whether performances in different areas share a common underlying trait. In the next chapter, I discuss some of these considerations regarding whether the differences observed in different areas of language should be described as "styles." Later, I discuss how thinking of individual differences as analytic versus holistic (or other terminology) sets us up for different types of explanations and how well those explanations have fared empirically.

For Further Reading

Several excellent reviews of this literature exist. I have made use of them as a starting point, and I encourage the interested reader to pursue them further: Bates, Bretherton, and Snyder (1988), Bretherton, McNew, Snyder, and Bates (1983), Goldfield and Snow (1989), and Nelson (1981, 1985).

Notes

1. There is some ambiguity about whether words are to be classified as naming things on the basis of *form* (i.e., nouns in the adult language) or on the basis of *function*. When a child demands "cookie," he or she is using a noun, but the pragmatic function is not one of reference—rather, it is a command. Because it is often difficult to discern function, researchers generally use form rather than function and categorize words in the early vocabulary as "common nouns" rather than "object names" (e.g., Bates et al., 1994; Lieven, Pine, & Barnes, 1992).

2. The early comprehender/nominal children in Rescorla's (1984) study were also initally likely to overextend a large number of words (e.g., to use "doggie" to

refer to a wide variety of animals). However, they soon learned the names of several members of the category and started using each word more narrowly.

3. Horgan (1980) found that 2- and 3-year-olds who were precocious in terms of MLU (mean length of utterance) concentrated on noun phrases, but the slower children performed better in comprehension. This may appear to contradict the tendency for referential children's comprehension to excel. However, her study is of 2- and 3-year-olds, whereas other studies are of 1- and 2-year-olds.

4. I have characterized the expressive-pronominal approach as relying fairly heavily on a holistic, unanalyzed approach to early sentences. There is some controversy over whether pronominal language involves productive usage or rote, unanalyzed forms. Bloom et al. (1975) argue that both nominal and pronominal utterances were productive (p. 34). However, Maratsos (1975) comments that "the periods where pronominal dominance is really marked are ones where expression of the relevant relations is often barely or marginally productive" (p. 92). Bates et al. (1988) also imply that early heavily pronominal language tends to be formulaic.

5. Another way that children may treat sound patterns holistically is in their attempts to simplify pronunciation of words. Some children use techniques to reduce the overall phonological complexity of a word (e.g., reduplication—"baba" for "bottle") or "repeating the salient syllable . . . of the whole word and then adding a stock element, often a syllable, to represent the rest of the word" (Ferguson, 1979, p. 196). Such techniques are reminiscent of dummy terms and pivot-open grammars discussed above.

3

Are There Styles of Language Development?

In the previous chapter, I described differences in the way that young children approach different aspects of language: semantics/vocabulary, grammar, phonology, and pragmatics. As I noted at the beginning of that chapter, researchers often suggest that a child's strategy in one aspect of language (e.g., lexical development) is paralleled in, for example, phonological development. When there are such linkages or similarities of approach in different areas, researchers begin to speak of different "styles" of language development. This term, style of development, has important implications. Instead of a stylistic pattern, the differences we observe could be separate, isolated dimensions of difference. They could be developmental differences rather than stylistic ones. In this chapter, I explore what the term "style" means in development and examine whether the individual differences we observe in language meet this definition.

Let me first summarize, from the research described in the previous chapter, the characteristics thought to coalesce into different styles of language development. In general, one style is thought to comprise referential early vocabulary, analytic approach to syntax, word or phonemic approach to phonology, and to focus on informational function of pragmatics. The other style, by contrast, comprises expressive early vocabulary, holistic approach to grammar, prosodic approach to phonology, and focuses on inter-personal function in pragmatics. (It is not always clear how risk taking vs. conservative characteristics "line up" with other ten-dencies.) A more detailed summary of contrasts between the styles is provided by Bates et al. (1988) and presented in Table 3.1.

As was seen in the previous chapter, these differences in children's language are labeled in a variety of ways: referential versus expres-sive, nominal versus pronominal, risk taking versus conservative, and analytic versus holistic. Why do we need to be careful about saying that these differences are "styles" of development, and if so, how do we label these styles? One reason is that it is very tempting to drift from "styles of development" to "types of children." Many child language researchers caution against this step (Bates et al., 1988, p. 66; Nelson, 1985, p. 123) and say that they are trying to describe *dimensions* that underlie the differences observed among children. Another reason to be careful about adopting a label for a style is the tendency to use (and possibly overuse) that label to think about the origins of individual differences in language—to jump from describing differences to explaining them. Before we make that jump, however, we need to ask some questions about whether the differences observed in children's language really constitute different styles.

What is implied if we call differences in behavior "stylistic"? Let me use a hypothetical example from a different area of behavior to help clarify this question. What would we mean if we described two different "styles" of social behavior, say, generosity versus selfishness? For one thing, we would mean that generosity and selfishness were alternatives, each with its *distinctive qualities*. We could say that "generous" behavior had certain social advantages and disadvantages, but that "selfish" behavior had pluses and minuses, too. Another thing we would mean by calling these "styles" is that generosity and selfishness are *generalized patterns of behavior*—children share/do not share a wide variety of things in a variety of situations (e.g., toys, food, space on a parent's lap). Furthermore, these "styles" of behavior would be likely to *persist over time*. A child who was generous at one point in time would

TABLE 3.1 Individual Differences in Language Development: Summary of Claims in the Literature

Strand 1	*Strand 2*
Semantics	
High proportion of nouns in first 50 words	Low proportion of nouns in first 50 words
Single words in early speech	Formulae in early speech
Imitates object names	Unselective imitation
Greater variety within lexical categories	Less variety within lexical categories
Meaningful elements only	Use of "dummy" words
High adjective use	Low adjective use
Context-flexible use of names	Context-bound use of names
Rapid vocabulary growth	Slower vocabulary growth
Grammar	
Telegraphic in Stage I	Inflections and function words in Stage I
Refers to self and others by name in Stage I	Refers to self and others by pronoun in Stage I
Noun-phrase expansion	Verb-phrase expansion
Morphological overgeneralization	Morphological undergeneralization
Consistent application of rules	Inconsistent application of rules
Novel combinations	Frozen forms
Imitation is behind spontaneous speech	Imitation is ahead of spontaneous speech
Fast learner	Slow learner
Pragmatics	
Object oriented	Person oriented
Declarative	Imperative
Low variety in speech acts	High variety in speech acts
Phonology	
Word oriented	Intonation oriented
High intelligibility	Low intelligibility
Segmental emphasis	Suprasegmental emphasis
Consistent pronunciation across word tokens	Variable pronunciation across word tokens
Demographic Variables	
Female	Male
Firstborn	Later-born
Higher SES	Lower SES

SOURCE: *From First Words to Grammar: Individual Differences and Dissociable Mechanisms* (Table 1) by E. Bates, I. Bretherton, and L. Snyder, 1988, Cambridge: Cambridge University Press. Copyright 1988 by Cambridge University Press. Adapted by permission.

likely be that way later. A related idea is that a "style" does not usually mean something that is a peculiarity of children in a particular developmental stage. We would not call a 20-month-old selfish because he or she has difficulty sharing objects—such reluctance is normal and typical of toddlers! Finally, a "style" is *distinct from developmental progress.* We would have to be very cautious in describing generous versus selfish styles in 2-year-olds, as it could be the case that the children who are being described as generous are the children who are simply making faster progress on their way out of the "terrible twos." To describe generosity and selfish *styles* in these children, we would have to show that they were *equivalent* in terms of their general socioemotional development. Styles are alternative ways of being at the same developmental level.

To summarize, first, a "style" is the child's preference, an option with its own distinctive character, strengths, and weaknesses. Second, a "style" is a generalized tendency that can be observed in a variety of behaviors. Therefore, behaviors thought to represent this general tendency should be correlated with one another. Third, styles are stable across time. Finally, stylistic differences should not reflect developmental level (Wolf & Grollman, 1982). To what extent do the individual differences observed in language meet these standards for being called styles? I take each of these criteria in turn.

Strengths and Weaknesses

When we talk about a "style," we usually think of a way of behaving that has its own distinctive character, its own strengths and weaknesses. Some authors have argued that we have not paid enough attention to characterizing the distinctive qualities of the expressive or holistic style (Lieven et al., 1992, p. 288). Expressive style is often defined simply as a relatively low level of common nouns in the early vocabulary. Consequently, instead of having two different styles, each with its own character, the researcher actually has a single score that represents how referential the subject is or is not.

Instead of characterizing expressiveness as an absence of refer-entiality, defining expressiveness in its own terms would facilitate thinking of the positive aspects of this approach. One could re-frame expressiveness in a way that values the role that formulaic speech plays in adult language and the role it may play in provid-ing an alternate route into multiword utterances (Lieven et al., 1992; Peters, 1983). The unique characteristics of expressiveness might be particularly well suited for learning languages other than English, those that combine morphemes rather than isolate them (Bloom et al., 1975, p. 34). An example of this approach is grouping variables into two different sets—the referential/nominal group and the expressive/pronominal group—each having its own defining characteristics. Studies employing this approach are described in the next section.

Generalized Patterns: Correlated Tendencies

A "style" is a generalized pattern of behavior. If different tasks are approached in the same way, then performance on those tasks ought to be correlated with one another. In the previous chapter, many points of connection were observed among different aspects of language (e.g., cases with both formulaic utterances and "mushy" articulation). However, there is as yet no strong empiri-cal evidence that the variations observed in one area of language tend to coincide with the variations observed in other aspects of language, such that there are two distinct sets of characteristics. It might be the case that, instead, there are "a number of sometimes correlated but logically independent variations" (Nelson, 1981, p. 179). It is important to realize that most of the studies that give rise to these composite portraits of two different styles involve a very small number of subjects, typically fewer than 20, and focus on only a few aspects of language.[1]

In such small samples, accidental associations of variables are quite possible. For example, if there are only 2 children in the study and the girl happens to be referential and the boy happens to be expressive, one should be very wary of concluding that gender is correlated with style—the association could be accidental. Small-sample research may also miss some important relationships—what if gender really did tend to go with style but both the boy and the girl you happened to study were referential (Hardy-Brown, 1983)? Because small samples might not happen to include individuals who show the general tendency, the results may be difficult to replicate (Hardy-Brown, 1983). Consequently, larger-scale correlational studies could be helpful in discerning stable relationships among language attributes.

Larger-scale (N = 30 and 87) correlational studies have been conducted on 20-month-olds. These studies provide evidence that variables that represent one "style" are more closely related to one another than they are to variables that represent the other "style." In other words, given a set of language variables, they tend to form distinct correlational "clumps" of interrelated behaviors. As expected, in both these studies, measures of reliance on nouns formed one factor, and measures of pronouns and function words formed another factor (Bretherton et al., 1983; Dixon & Shore, 1991a, 1991b, 1992, 1993).[2] If no styles existed, either all the variables would tend to be related to all the other variables (representing some generalized overall language ability) or none of the variables would relate to each other (indicating that all these variables tap separate skills). Further analyses in Dixon and Shore (1992, 1993) showed that these two factors made a better fit to the data than a single general language ability factor made up of all of the variables.

However, to account for all variability in the different aspects of language, more than two factors may be needed (Bates et al., 1988, p. 55). In fact, in addition to the nominal-referential factor and the pronouns and grammatical morpheme cluster, Bretherton et al. (1983) found another one or two clusters involving labeling and imitation rates and decontextualized use of language.[3] Further detail about this sample is described below in the section titled "Persistence Over Time."

An important feature of these studies is that they have not grouped *children* into nominal versus pronominal styles. In the Dixon and Shore studies, for example, each child received *two* factor scores: One was a composite of performance on the referential/nominal factor, and the other represented performance on the expressive/pronominal factor. It was possible to be high or low on both. Using correlational techniques, such as factor and cluster analysis, recognizes the unique features of each style and suggests that all children may possess both types of characteristics to some degree. The results also suggest that referential-analytic skills and expressive-holistic skills may not be the only dimensions of difference among toddlers' language abilities.

These larger-scale studies found considerable evidence of links between children's approach to vocabulary-semantic development and their approach to grammar. Compared to lexical-grammatical development, about which we have learned a good deal, we know much less about how these areas are related to phonology and pragmatics. One of the consequences is that we have little information about how (or whether) the risk taking versus conservative dimension, which has primarily been described for the development of the phonological system, intersects with the analytic versus holistic dimension, which has primarily been described in lexical and grammatical development. We do not know, for example, whether referential-nominal-analytic children would be described as "conservative" in terms of developing their phonological systems. The relationships between pragmatics and semantic development are a matter of some controversy as well, as discussed in the previous chapter. We do not know if the nominal-pronominal distinction in vocabulary coincides with referential versus expressive pragmatic functions. Future work needs to address the relationships among these domains.

Persistence Over Time

When we call something a "style" of behavior or development, we not only mean that it has its own distinctive character and that it is generalized over situations but also that it persists for some time. To what extent do the individual differences observed in language remain characteristic of children's language acquisition over a period of time?

This turns out to be a multifaceted question. To answer it, we need to explore not only the time course or history of language development but also the effects of situational factors on language use. As will be seen, the type of early vocabulary that children use appears to be related to their early approach to grammar. As children progress beyond the initial steps, however, they tend to begin making greater use of forms/strategies from the complementary approach. This means that these individual differences will be most apparent below MLU of 2.0, which for most children covers roughly the second year of life, up until about 2.5 years. However, some remnants of the child's early preference may remain in later language-using tasks. I then consider situational factors because some case studies indicate that children's strategy can shift with situation (to some extent) or with learning a new language.

CONTINUITY OF STYLE INTO MULTIWORD SPEECH AND PRODUCTIVE CONTROL OVER GRAMMAR

Considerable evidence suggests that children who are referential in their early vocabulary tend to take a nominal approach to early multiword utterances and that expressive vocabulary predicts pronominal-style early multiword utterances (e.g., Hampson, 1989; Nelson, 1975; Starr, 1975). Although Bauer (1985) showed some children changing style classification over a 6-week period in early multiword speech, this instability may be a result of using a dichotomous (either-or) type of categorization. Dixon and Shore (1993) reanalyzed these data, together with another sample, and showed that children's referential and expressive multiword speech composite scores at 20 months tended to be correlated with those scores 6 weeks later.

It is fairly straightforward to explain how a nominal-analytic strategy could lead to acquiring productive control over function words and inflections (e.g., prepositions, "-ing"). Productive control means that each element in the utterance is understood to be separate and can be recombined in many ways with other words (e.g., "*the* doggie" and "*the* bus"). A child with a nominal-analytic bias is particularly good at isolating these component parts of utterances for later recombination. Consequently, a child might easily retain this preference from early vocabulary through early multiword utterances into productive grammar. However, there is some controversy over whether an early reliance on formulaic utterances can lay the groundwork for productive use of function words and inflections. Some research indicates that one can see a link between early frozen phrases and the beginnings of more sophisticated utterances (Nelson, 1973, p. 79). Lieven et al. (1992) found that a high use of frozen phrases (at the 100-word vocabulary point) was positively related to the achievement of a number of "potentially productive utterances." They also found that phrases were negatively related to use of nouns. This is consistent with the view that phrases and nouns are alternative means of achieving a given level of sophistication and suggests that the use of phrases can be a valuable strategy in language development (Lieven et al., 1992).

However, other authors question the relationship between early expressive-style variables and productive control of grammar. In a large survey study of vocabulary growth, children who produced few common nouns in the first 50 words were not necessarily advanced at closed-class usage 6.5 months later. This suggests that children who probably relied on phrases and personal-social words in their early vocabulary do not necessarily come to *productive* use of all the little words that make up those phrases any earlier than do other children. At least in early language development, "advanced" children did not necessarily use more or fewer function words. This is consistent with the idea that early use of these forms represents unanalyzed rote processes and that early closed-class usage is not related to achieving productive control over grammatical morphemes (Bates et al., 1994).

The discrepancy between the Lieven et al. results and those of Bates et al. may be due to differences in measurement—Bates et al. apparently did not directly assess frozen phrases as part of the early vocabulary, whereas Lieven et al. did. Consequently, it is still possible that, as Lieven et al. suggest, *both* common nouns and frozen phrases show developmental increases and that these types

are in opposition at the 50- and 100-word points in early vocabulary development.

A COMPARISON OF LARGE SAMPLE
AND INDIVIDUAL RESEARCH ON CONTINUITY

Bates et al. (1988) argue that one can trace stylistic development
from early vocabulary through the beginnings of productivity.
Essentially, they followed an "analytic approach" strand of language variables all the way from early comprehension through
open-class vocabulary expansion at 20 months to productive morphology at 28 months. By contrast, "rote or formulaic" variables
do not form a continuous longitudinal strand, but they are distinct
from "analytic" variables at each age level. It is interesting to
compare their findings to those of Rescorla (1984), who studied
six children over roughly the same time frame. Her case examples
show very interesting similarities to the "composite portrait" obtained from Bates et al.'s larger-sample data. To see this interesting
congruence, it is necessary to present each of their findings in
some detail.

I turn first to Bates et al. (1988), who report on several studies
of a longitudinal sample of 27 middle-class infants who were seen
at 10, 13, 20, and 28 months. At each age point, both home and lab
visits were conducted with the infants and consisted of a variety
of structured and unstructured tasks. These tasks were designed
to assess many aspects of sensorimotor and symbolic abilities,
such as causality, imitation, and symbolic play. The parents were
also interviewed about their infants' language progress. Bates et al.
believe that at 10 and 13 months, the contextual flexibility of object
words indicates that the child understands that things have
names. In addition, 10-month comprehension predicted the number of nouns and contextually flexible nouns that children produced at 13 months. These variables formed the basis of an
"analytic" strand of variables, which they traced through to 28
months. From these beginnings, 13-month comprehension and
flexible noun production predicted 20-month clusters of variables
that had to do with using language in a semantically and prag-

matically flexible way. Thirteen-month referential-analytic variables predicted at 20 months not noun vocabulary but expansion of open-class vocabulary in general.[4] These lexical beginnings have implications for productive grammar at 28 months. Analytic variables, such as 13-month comprehension and flexible noun production, and 20-month vocabulary predicted 28-month MLU as well as measures of children's comprehension and production of grammatical morphemes at 28 months.

In contrast to these referential-analytic variables, MLU and the use of function words and inflections at 20 months related back to *total* production at 13 months. Bates et al. argue that high MLU at 20 months is a result of "loading" one's utterances with elements the child does not yet really understand and is continuous with rote unanalyzed production from the beginning. Further evidence that holistic/rote processes are implicated in 20-month MLU is that it predicted neither 28-month MLU nor grammatical morpheme comprehension and production.

Bates et al. (1988) believe that these results are supportive of a strong developmental link between grammar and semantics. They argue that at 13 months the most advanced children are acquiring object names, at 20 months they are expanding all aspects of the open class, and at 28 months they are acquiring productive morphology by the same processes used to acquire any lexical items. However, there are evidently some children who take an alternate route to success. "Verb specialization seems to have a kind of optional status, a 'booster rocket' some children use . . . to catch up (at least temporarily) with those children who have exploited the use of lexical-conceptual analysis at every stage" (pp. 161-162).

I turn now to Rescorla (1984), who provides remarkable support of this picture on the basis of her multiple-case study of six children. It is refreshing to see individuals whose development resembles the composite portraits constructed from a group of children's data. Rescorla would agree with Bates et al. that early comprehension is highly predictive of later linguistic development. Three children in her sample could be described as early comprehenders. All three (plus one of the later comprehenders, who will be discussed shortly) had a high proportion of nouns in their early comprehension vocabularies.

When the children were 2 years old, the early comprehenders excelled on a number of indices of grammatical development. Interestingly, one "slow comprehender" had almost caught up with the more advanced children. This was the child who, although her overall comprehension was low, comprehended a high proportion of nouns. Two things are of particular interest, given Bates et al.'s description of their 20-month sample: This child had a high verb density per utterance (higher than two of the early comprehenders) and had an overall vocabulary count approaching that of the early comprehender group. This is consistent with Bates et al.'s claims that the more advanced children in their sample were characterized by early noun comprehension and a 20-month vocabulary that involved expansion of the open class. It also supports their claim that some children at 20 months used verb density as a "booster rocket" to catch up with the more advanced children.

CONVERGENCE OF STYLES

There is considerable evidence that stylistic variations tend to converge as children begin to acquire productive control over morphology (i.e., as MLU approaches 2.0, typically about 2.5 years of age). Convergence of style has been observed since the original samples studied by Nelson and Bloom. Over time, the pronominal speakers in Bloom et al.'s (1975) group increased their nominal usage and the nominal speakers increased their pronominal usage (pp. 20, 24). The children from Nelson's 1973 study were followed up by home visits at 24 and 30 months. Referential speakers' early utterances contained a high proportion of nouns compared to pronouns. They named the objects they were talking about, they used a variety of nouns, and their early sentences frequently involved object modifiers, such as adjectives and possessives. With development, they began to rely more heavily on pronouns and decreased the number of nouns they used. Expressive speakers, by contrast, initially had more balanced proportions of nouns and pronouns. Their use of pronouns remained relatively stable over time, but they showed a large increase in noun use. Their language increasingly employed individual words for specific things (Nelson, 1975, pp. 475-476).

The same convergence has been observed in French-acquiring children (Lightbown, 1973, cited in Bloom & Lahey, 1978, p. 171) and when different defining characteristics are used to classify children into style groups: nominal versus pronominal multiword examples provided by parents in an interview (Bauer, 1985) and even imitation rather than lexical or grammatical preference (Nelson, Baker, Denniger, Bonvillian, & Kaplan, 1985, p. 443).

DO LANGUAGE STYLES EXTEND
BEYOND THE EARLY STAGES OF ACQUISITION?

Only sporadic data are available, and these often provide contradictory answers to our questions about further development in the lexicon, in grammar, and in pragmatics. We might ask whether a tendency to rely on and elaborate nouns and noun phrases persists into the period of productive control over function words. A study of 2- and 3-year-olds found distinctions between the speech of "noun lovers" and that of "noun leavers," even though these children were older and had higher MLUs than the age range in which stylistic differences are typically seen (Horgan, 1980, p. 10). However, at 28 months, children whose vocabularies had many nouns did not necessarily also have many other noun-phrase relevant parts of speech, such as articles and adjectives (Bates et al., 1988).

In the grammatical arena, we might wonder whether children continue to employ a frozen phrase strategy, even as they are acquiring productive control over at least some morphemes. Formulaic or gestalt strategies do appear in the third year, lending credence to the idea that language styles persist for some period of time (Clark, 1974; Peters, 1977).

What about pragmatics—do early language styles leave traces in children's social use of language? In a referential-communication task, children are asked to describe novel objects so that a listener can select them from an array. One might expect nominal-referential children to excel at object description. But these tasks also involve sensitivity to the listener's needs, so one might expect expressive children to do well. Contradictory findings have been reported by Horgan (1980), who found her 5-year-old noun "lovers" to be more efficient in their descriptions than the "leavers," and by Nelson et al. (1985), who report that 4.5-year-olds who had been previously classified as expressive gave more effective descriptions than their referential counterparts. However, Horgan describes the noun leavers as being more sensitive to nonlinguistic context and social demands than the noun lovers, so the issue remains unclear.

WITHIN-CHILD CONSISTENCY ACROSS SITUATIONS

If differences in language represent the manifestation of some underlying, enduring characteristic, the child's approach to language should be relatively consistent across situations. However, some data indicate that there is variability *within* a given child.

Context can affect the tendency to produce unintelligible utterances. One author reports that her subject tended to speak more clearly in labeling situations and more unintelligibly in conversational situations (Peters, 1977). In contrast, Vihman et al. (1986) say that children may engage in more unintelligible vocalizations when they are alone than when in a conversation.

Context can also affect the preferences of referential and expressive children for informational versus interpersonal language uses. In a routine caretaking situation, 2-year-olds who used many nouns concentrated on object-oriented functions, whereas children who produced more pronominal forms concentrated on personal and instrumental functions. However, when playing with a novel castle toy, these differences were less pronounced, indicating that in an object-oriented situation children will increase their use of referential functions (Lucariello & Nelson, described by Nelson, 1985, p. 113).

However, some stylistic tendencies do appear to be consistent across contexts. Twenty-month-olds' spontaneous reliance on nouns (as a percentage of total words produced) was consistent across food and play situations. None of the 18 children studied was classified as expressive in one situation and referential in the other (Hampson & Nelson, 1993).

CHILDREN ACQUIRING A SECOND LANGUAGE

A small number of reports describe a child shifting strategies from referential to expressive to acquire a second language. Julia's acquisition of English (see Chapter 2) was referential-analytic. When Julia was 20 to 24 months old she and her parents were in Rome, where her primary opportunity to learn Italian occurred during lunch with her baby-sitter's parents. At the end of the stay, her Italian vocabulary consisted of only 24% common nouns, and those that she did know were recognizably embedded in social rituals surrounding lunchtime! Vihman's daughter was also analytic in learning her first language but gestalt in learning her second at age 2 (personal communication reported in Peters, 1977).

Why might children take such a different approach to learning their second language at age 2? A number of different possibilities have been proposed, some of which have to do with second language learning and others with age. Perhaps the structure of the language being acquired makes a particular style more efficient for acquisition (Peters, 1977). Although this is possible, it does not seem to meet the current case. Vihman's daughter (and Fillmore's subjects below) switched to an expressive style to learn English, and if either of the two styles has an advantage in learning English, it is most likely the referential style.

Another language-oriented explanation takes note of the formulaic utterances observed in Fillmore's (1979) study of early grade-school-aged children learning English as a second language. Perhaps a formulaic strategy is common to children learning their second language by sudden immersion (Bates et al., 1988), just as a tourist phrase book can be useful upon first arrival in a foreign country. A related idea is that children who already have a language do not need the second language for the internal cognitive purpose of representing the world—instead, they need the second language to get along socially. This may bias them toward a gestalt strategy (Peters, 1983, p. 22).

Alternative explanations for style switching suggest that beginning a language in your third year is a different ballgame than starting in your first year. In addition to having more mature memory abilities, 2-year-olds may receive longer utterances as input than do younger children (Bates et al., 1988, p. 259; Peters, 1977). These factors taken together could make a formulaic approach the tool of choice. At this point, it is not known which of these factors are responsible for these children's style switching or whether these factors would apply to other children.

SUMMARY AND IMPLICATIONS

There is reasonable evidence to suggest that these individual differences characterize children's early approaches to vocabulary and multiword combinations at least into the third year. It also appears that we can follow an "analytic" route for acquisition from early evidence of comprehension through the beginnings of productive control over grammatical morphemes. However, there is some controversy over whether an early reliance on formulaic utterances can lay the groundwork for grammatical productivity.

As children progress beyond the initial steps, they tend to begin making greater use of forms/strategies from the complementary approach. Children who had previously concentrated on isolating content words and combining them now begin to bring those skills to bear on the "little words." Children who had previously worked with holistic general phrases, such as "dat mine," begin to split these apart, recombine them, and make them more specific (e.g., "dat bear mine"). It is not certain whether the child's early preference will be evident in later language-using tasks, such as referential communication.

Although children's approach to early language acquisition shows consistency over at least the second year of life, some case studies indicate that children's strategy can shift with a given situation or with learning a new language. These observations suggest that "style" should not be thought of as an either-or phenomenon. Rather, it appears that children have both of these sets of tools available to them. Although they tend to rely on one set over the other, context can also influence their selection.

Relation to General Developmental Level

Are the "stylistic" differences observed in language ways of being at the same level of sophistication, or are they differences in rate of progression along a common pathway? Although general chattiness (the sheer frequency of the child's talking) does not appear to be related to style (Nelson, 1973, p. 47), some authors argue that individual differences in language are related to overall linguistic progress (Nelson, 1985, p. 119). Other authors disagree, preferring to believe that stylistic differences represent relative strengths in equally necessary skills (Bates et al., 1988, p. 241). They present evidence that differences between style groups are not in overall rate of language development but, rather, in the relative balance and preferences among different aspects of language (Nelson et al., 1985, p. 446).

The issue of general developmental progress is discussed for overall *language* development and for vocabulary and syntax in particular and for developmental level in *intelligence*. As will be seen, it appears that neither style is necessarily advantaged in overall language development in terms of either vocabulary or grammatical complexity. Although the evidence on intelligence is scanty, what little there is suggests that intelligence is not the underlying basis for referentiality.

VOCABULARY

The relationship between referential style and vocabulary development is somewhat controversial at the present time. In Nelson's original study, the referential children showed greater acceleration of vocabulary learning just prior to reaching 50 words and a more rapid rate of vocabulary acquisition in the first 50 words. By age 2, vocabulary count was substantially higher for referential children (Nelson, 1973, pp. 39, 40). Children who show a vocabulary burst are most likely adding primarily nouns. However, a substantial minority show a more gradual vocabulary increase that is balanced between nouns and other types of words (Goldfield & Reznick, 1990).

Critics, however, react negatively to the idea that referential style is associated with rate advantages in vocabulary development (e.g., Hampson & Nelson, 1993, p. 323). They argue that this conclusion arises from methodology that confounds stylistic differences with developmental differences, and that level of vocabulary must be controlled before style differences can be claimed. Two recent studies (one involving 14 infants, the other involving 200 infants) have found that some vocabulary changes are associated with *developmental* changes as opposed to *stylistic* differences. First, there was an average increase in proportion of referential vocabulary from the 25-word vocabulary level to the 50-word level. Consequently, an increase in general nominals is a developmental feature of language acquisition that cuts across style (Pine & Lieven, 1990). Second, there was no relationship between referential vocabulary at 50 words and age at 50 words in either Nelson's (1973) study or Pine and Lieven's (1990) results. Furthermore, if referential style is associated with rapid vocabulary development, one would expect children with high degrees of referential style to be relatively younger than other children at their vocabulary level. Parental reports of vocabulary for over 200 infants showed the opposite tendency! Low referential children tended to be younger (i.e., more precocious). These researchers also found that referential style in the 10- to 50-word period did not predict total vocabulary approximately 6.5 months later (Bates et al., 1994).

These more recent studies argue that "when vocabulary levels are controlled, the oft-cited association between referential style and precocity seems to disappear." (Bates et al., 1994, p. 117). Similarly, although some children in Bloom's (1993) study showed a dramatic vocabulary spurt (p. 189), their learning of nouns did not show a simultaneous increase (L. Bloom, personal communication, December 1993). It is hard to know how to resolve this controversy. It appears that general nominals show both developmental change and stylistic differences. When one controls for vocabulary level, it appears that referential children may show more of a "naming burst" just prior to 50 words, and perhaps this rate advantage persists for a time. However, it appears that by the middle of the third year this discrepancy disappears.

Some possible support for this idea comes from an examination of data provided by Goldfield and Reznick (1990). They found that the percentage of nouns in the vocabulary tended to increase over time in children who experienced a growth spurt in vocabulary *and* those who did not (similar to Lieven & Pine and Bates et al.). However, children who experienced a spurt tended to have a higher average number of nouns in their early vocabularies (under 80 words). Are the nominal spurters precocious in terms of overall vocabulary development? A visual examination of their figures suggests that the two groups (nominal spurters vs. more balanced vocabulary nonspurters) were about the same *mean* age at 50 words, although there was more variation, not surprisingly, in the spurting group. However, it appears that at 100 words the spurters may have been a little younger. This supports the idea that somewhere between 18 months and 2 years, nominal children are "on a roll" in terms of vocabulary acquisition and may enjoy a temporary advantage.

SYNTAX

Some studies suggest that children's rate of acquisition is related to their referential versus expressive strategy, which would suggest that expressive children are simply slower versions of the referential pattern. For example, Bloom (1973, pp. 115-119) and Leonard (1976, p. 43) note that in pivot-open structures the relational word relies on the content word to carry the burden of the meaning. In telegraphic utterances, each word makes more of an independent contribution to the meaning of the sentence. One could therefore argue that pivot-open structures are less "differentiated" and so less developmentally advanced (Werner & Kaplan, 1963, pp. 147-148).

Two studies show expressive children to be disadvantaged in moving into syntax. In a comparison of two children, the expressive child started using words later and his one-word stage lasted about 2 months longer than the more referential child's did (Dore, 1974). Expressive strategies, such as presence of dummy forms, consistent use of English word order, and small variety of sentence types in early syntax, have been also related to a slower rate of developing syntax (Ramer, 1976).

To make the claim that these differences are developmental rather than stylistic, one would have to show that the less advanced children become more like the more advanced ones when they get further along, or that children *equated for syntactic level* do not differ in these ways. Some problems arise in this analysis. I take each of these claims in turn.

First, do expressive-style speakers grow up to be referential-style speakers? The longitudinal data reviewed above make the progression sound more like a convergence rather than making the expressive children look more like the referential children. Furthermore, if expressivity is simply early/delayed language development, we should see late talkers first showing signs of being expressive and later coming to look more like referential children. Alternatively, perhaps they would skip the expressive "stage" and join up with their age mates as referential speakers. Earlier speakers may be more likely to show style differences in their first 50 words, whereas those who reach the 50-word point between 18 and 21 months may be less likely to do so (Nelson, 1985, p. 117). Although the late starters may be less likely to evidence stylistic variation, both styles are still available to them, indicating that referential versus expressive tendencies are not simply a result of precocious language development (Hampson & Nelson, 1993).

Second, do children at the same level of syntactic development show stylistic differences? In dealing with this issue, most researchers have asked the question the other way around—do referential versus expressive groups of children differ in terms of utterance complexity? Several studies indicate that the answer is no, even when style groups are defined in a number of different ways: first 50-word vocabulary (Nelson, 1973, p. 40), observed noun-to-total-word ratio (Hampson & Nelson, 1990, 1993), predominance of noun-noun versus pronoun or no-noun utterances in interview examples of multiword speech (Bauer, 1984), and imitative-referential versus personal social-syntactic-low imitating style (Nelson et al., 1985). A variety of measures of utterance complexity and length have been used, including MLU, verb complexity, and function words. Even when style is defined as a dimension rather than a typology, the same results obtain. Referential style assessed between 10 and 50 words was not predictive of utterance complexity assessed approximately 6.5 months later (Bates et al., 1994).

A difficult and subtle problem in disentangling developmental changes from stylistic differences is finding a measure of developmental change that does not already presuppose that the behaviors characteristic of a particular style are more advanced. The measure of developmental progress (e.g., syntactic development) needs to be impartial. The most widely known and used estimate of overall syntactic development is MLU. However, questions have been raised about whether MLU is stylistically unbiased. Charges have been raised that MLU overlooks the variety in "noun leavers" utterances (Horgan, 1980, p. 10), or the number of sentences they use (Nelson, 1975, p. 470), giving the appearance that their language is less advanced. Other critics argue that morphemes and utterances, the basic units for computing MLU, are problematic, particularly considering gestalt language (Branigan, 1976, p. 68; Plunkett, 1993). Because MLU was developed in a study of "firstborn mainstream American children chosen for their volubility and intelligibility," the units for computing it "may not necessarily apply to other children, or to the same children at different stages, or even to the same child in different utterances" (Peters, 1983, p. 96).

INTELLIGENCE

Some might argue that individual differences in language are really just a by-product of IQ and that smart children are referential children. This is not the place to discuss all the complex issues surrounding the definition and measurement of intelligence. My focus is on issues that bear directly on the problem at hand. One set of problems has to do with measuring intelligence in this age range, and a second set has to do with measuring intelligence in a way that is not already stylistically biased.

Age is a problem in that the individual differences in language that I have been discussing all take place before 3 years of age. To make a long story short, not many measures before 3 years of age (with the exception of infant speed-of-habituation measures) predict performance on later intelligence tests (Honzik, 1983; McCall, 1983). There are standardized developmental tests for infants, such as the Bayley, and tests of Piagetian sensorimotor cognitive accomplishments, but performance on these does not predict performance on later IQ tests. Although these tests do not predict later tested intelligence, they may give us some idea of the child's general developmental progress. In one study, early comprehending-referential style children tended to have higher Bayley MDI scores at 12 and 24 months (Rescorla, 1984). However, there is evidence that referential and expressive groups of children do not differ on Piagetian achievements such as means-ends, causality, and object permanence (Bauer, 1984, 1985). Even if we *had* a consistent association between language style and infant mental development measures, we would have no guarantee that language style was associated with what we later count as intelligence.

The other set of problems involves measuring "intelligence" in a way that does not implicitly advantage children who tend to rely on particular cognitive/linguistic strategies. The analytic-nominal skills associated with the referential child tend to be the type of intelligence that is assessed and valued in school. However, this emphasis may reflect a biased view of intelligence (Horgan, 1980; Nelson, 1981). One study of six children did show a connection between early comprehending-referential-style children and higher Binet IQ scores at age 3. However, the Binet test relies heavily on verbal abilities and may emphasize the skills at which referential-analytic children excel. It is unclear whether their language comprehension facilitated their intelligence or vice versa or whether both were influenced by a third factor (Rescorla, 1984).

One study that made an effort to disentangle these used the Peabody Picture Vocabulary Test (PPVT)· and the total verbal output at 28 months as controls for "general intelligence" and talkativeness. In other words, to whatever extent "intelligence tests" are biased toward referential skills, that influence was statistically removed. The researchers found that the measures that were characteristic of referential-analytic style (from lexical-semantic development at 13 and 20 months to 28-month measures of syntactic development) still formed a coherent correlational pattern. The stylistic association of the referential-analytic variables was not a result of a heavily verbal measure of "intelligence" (Bates et al., 1988).

Given the larger sample (30 children in the Bates et al. study compared to six in Rescorla's) and the statistical control in Bates et al., it appears that referential style is not an artifact of greater intelligence. To my knowledge, there is no longitudinal evidence about the relationship between linguistic style and standard intelligence tests beyond 3 years of age. Ideally, we would obtain a variety of measures of cognitive abilities, preferably nonverbal, to assess the intelligence of children who started out with a referential/expressive linguistic strategy.

SUMMARY AND IMPLICATIONS

If it were true that "language style" characteristics were associated with general intelligence or language ability, it would seriously undermine the notion of two qualitatively different approaches to language acquisition. This is a difficult and complex issue for a number of reasons. One problem is determining whether differences between children are due to style or due to development, especially when the way the style manifests itself changes with age! Disentangling these sources of difference generally involves large-scale longitudinal studies, which are very rare. A more subtle problem is defining what is meant by developmental progress in a stylistically nonbiased way. MLU is questionable, and a reliable measure of intelligence does not exist in this age range.

Although there is uncertainty, I think that neither style necessarily has an advantage in overall linguistic development. Although referential children may have an early advantage in
vocabulary acquisition, this gap may disappear. Referential versus expressive groups of children do not show an average difference on several different measures of utterance complexity. With
increasing development, it appears that *both* styles tend to incorporate elements of the other rather than one catching up with the
other. Furthermore, Bates et al. (1988) find two or more orthogonal
(uncorrelated) language factors at each point in their longitudinal
study. This suggests qualitative differences, as shared variance
could be attributable to some underlying general development
factor. Finally, it appears that referential style is not simply a result
of greater intelligence. From the evidence at hand, I think it is at
least as possible that language styles are independent of developmental level as that they are a result of it.

Are There Styles of Language Development?

We do not really know. There are no longitudinal, correlational
data on a sufficient sample size of children that cover semantic,
syntactic, phonological, and pragmatic development controlling
for level of overall language development and general intelligence
(if there is such a thing). That said, a case can be made that
individual differences in language development may meet the
criteria to be called "styles."

We can describe at least two different styles in ways that show
their *unique qualities.* Language development styles are *generalized
tendencies* in that children's early approach to vocabulary is related
to their early approach to grammar, and at present, the variables
that we have observed to coalesce could probably be described as
"analytic" versus "holistic" in theme. When more data are obtained about how individual differences in phonological and
pragmatic development relate to lexical and grammatical development, this characterization might change. We may find that two
"styles" are not enough to describe the variations we see. It is

possible, for example, that the risk taking versus conservative dimension is orthogonal to whether the child concentrates on analysis or holistic processing. Although infants' approach to language appears to *persist over time* at least into their third year of life, it also appears that children thereafter begin to increase their reliance on the nonpreferred mode. Such convergence is one piece of evidence, among others, that stylistic differences *do not reduce simply to developmental change.*

If there are styles of language development, how should we characterize them? As mentioned above, typologies are problematic. One way of avoiding categories of children is to think of the differences as a continuum—there are highly analytic children at one end and highly holistic children at the other, with most children falling somewhere in between. Another way is to think of *two* continuua: from very low analytic to very high analytic and from very low holistic to very high holistic. The "classic" referential-analytic child would be high on the analytic dimension and low on the holistic dimension. The "classic" expressive-holistic child would have the opposite pattern. It would be possible to be high, medium, or low on both.

This picture is more complicated than a typology or a single continuum, but it has some advantages. One advantage is that both of these dimensions are positive characteristics. Because languages not only are rule governed but also contain many "exceptions to the rule" and must simply be memorized, *both* forms of processing are necessary and useful for successful acquisition (Bates et al., 1988, p. 241). When we have only a single dimension, we frequently ask "Which one is better?" More than one dimension makes it possible to be smart in different ways and so fits better with the more multifaceted quality of recent thinking about the nature of intelligence.

Another advantage is in fit with the data. The multidimensional approach is congruent with the large-scale studies that find two or more clusters of correlated variables. It also makes more sense of the convergence-of-style phenomenon—if there were only one dimension a child would have to become less nominal-analytic in order to increase pronominal-holistic performance. Finally, it is easier to explain context sensitivity with multiple dimensions. In a single continuum model, referential and expressive strategies would be mutually exclusive. In a multidimensional approach, each child could have *both* types of abilities, with a typical balance or preference between them, that could change as the situation required. Consequently, although we often use the shorthand of talking about "referential" and "expressive" children, it is probably more accurate to describe them respectively as "children who are relatively skilled at analysis and less so at holistic processes" and "children who are relatively skilled at holistic processes and less so at analysis."

Notes

1. A "large" study of phonological development is that of Vihman, Ferguson, and Elbert (1986) with 10 subjects—it is more common to have three or fewer subjects (e.g., Clark, 1974; Macken, 1978; Peters, 1977; Stoel-Gammon & Cooper, 1984; Vihman, 1981). All the "classic" studies of syntax (Bloom, 1970; Bloom, Lightbown, & Hood, 1975; Ramer, 1976) have fewer than 10 subjects. Similarly, most major studies of semantic/pragmatic development (Dore, 1974; Goldfield & Reznick, 1990; Lieven, 1978; Nelson, 1973, 1975; Rescorla, 1984) have 18 or fewer subjects.

2. In the Dixon and Shore study, body parts vocabulary (as an indicator of general vocabulary) and multiword utterances with two nouns were strongly related to a referential/nominal factor. The expressive/pronominal factor was made up of multiword utterances containing pronouns only, neither nouns nor pronouns, and/or morphological elements, such as inflections, articles, auxiliaries, or prepositions.

3. There were both maternal interview and observational language variables on 30 children at 20 months in Bretherton, McNew, Snyder, and Bates's (1983) study. Parents were asked how the child used language to engage in conversation, to label objects, to imitate others, to talk about absent objects, and to use articles, prepositions, and inflections. Parents were also asked about different types of multiword combinations: pivot-open structures, noun-noun combinations, and one noun plus another content word.

4. One would have expected that these referential-analytic variables would also predict a high proportion of noun-noun combinations. However, this was not the case. Instead, Bates et al. suggest that telegraphic speech (including noun-noun combinations) at 20 months represents a developmental rather than stylistic advance—the emergence of memory ability to "chunk" two or more elements in working memory.

4

Explanations for
Individual Differences
in Language Development

Why do children show different patterns of language development? Many different explanations have been proposed. Explanations run the entire range of developmental mechanisms, from rate of maturation of brain areas to social class. I discuss several of these in turn, together with whatever relevant data are available. These are organized in a rough sequence from external factors to internal factors. I first consider broad environmental factors and then a variety of possible social influences. A hybrid social/cognitive model then precedes a discussion of potential cognitive underpinnings for language style. Internal factors such as motivation and temperament are considered, and finally, language-specific (biological) bases are discussed.

This chapter is necessarily somewhat speculative because causation is difficult to demonstrate for phenomena like these. First of all, we cannot do experiments (e.g., randomly assigning infants to different parents), so we are left to correlational methodologies that do not allow causal conclusions. Second, studies of children with their biological parents inevitably confound genetic and environmental influences, so most studies cannot disentangle these potentially causal factors. Third, we tend to think of parental behavior as the cause and of children's behavior as the effect—but it could be true that characteristics of the child influence the parent's behavior.

Additional methodological problems hinder firm conclusions. Often it is difficult to operationalize the constructs that we think are important—what exactly do we mean by "responsive" parenting or by "analytic" skills in infants? It is also hard to measure these characteristics in an unobtrusive way—anytime we observe parents and infants in the home or lab, their behavior might be distorted by our presence. Furthermore, people tend to behave somewhat differently in different situations, and our choice of situation(s) in which to observe parents and infants may affect their interaction. Finally, once again, most of the studies reported in this literature involve very small samples. Findings of correlations in small samples could be accidental associations and be hard to replicate. I have tried to give more weight to evidence from the "larger" samples, whenever it is available, but even these generally have fewer than 50 subjects. Consequently, instead of this chapter being about causes of language style differences, it is better described as a survey of hypotheses about the sources of children's stylistic preferences and as a summary of factors that have been fairly consistently associated with language style.

General Environmental Explanations

RELATIONS TO GENDER, BIRTH ORDER, AND SOCIOECONOMIC STATUS

Referential-analytic and expressive-holistic qualities remind us of other distinctions between children. People frequently ask "Is language style related to gender?" because the personal-social phrases associated with the expressive dimension remind them of the interpersonal sensitivity we culturally associate with girls. Or they will think of how much time the parents of firstborns feel they spend "teaching" the baby the names of things and ask if language style is associated with birth order. They may also wonder whether the academic orientation of middle-class families may be conducive to referential-analytic style.

Gender and Birth Order

When there is an association between gender and language style, in case studies or small samples generally girls are referential and boys expressive. However, samples larger than 12 tend to find either no style differences or style differences between children of the same gender.[1]

When language style differences are associated with birth order, firstborns tend to be referential, whereas expressive infants are more likely to be laterborns. Parents' everyday experience suggests that firstborns and laterborns may experience different language learning environments (Nelson, 1985, p. 107; Nelson et al., 1985). However, the evidence of an association between birth order and language style is equivocal. A comparable number of studies with comparable sample sizes find opposite trends or no birth order effects.[2]

Socioeconomic Status

Social class differences in language development may exist and be related to language style. Middle-class infants tend to be more responsive to language and to engage in more object naming than do lower-class infants. Finally, middle-class mothers tend to be more verbally responsive, to provide more complex linguistic models, and to have higher linguistic expectations of their toddlers than do lower-class mothers (reviewed by Golden & Birns, 1976).[3]

These social class differences parallel differences between linguistic styles (e.g., sensitivity to language as medium) and object naming. This analogy makes it tempting to suggest that language/ parenting patterns associated with social class are at least partly responsible for language acquisition styles. The relationship between caregiver style/linguistic input and child acquisition style is discussed in more detail below. However, social class alone cannot be the whole story because most of the time linguistic style differences have been found in children from the *same* social class.

OTHER CHARACTERISTICS

Referential children were more likely than expressive children to have and enjoy playing with books, records, and manipulative toys (Nelson, 1973, pp. 58-63; Rescorla, 1984, p. 109). There was also a modest tendency in Nelson's (1973) study for unemployed mothers to have referential children. Higher parent education and intellectual atmosphere of the home have also been related to referential style (pp. 58-63; Rescorla, 1984, p. 109).

CRITIQUE OF GENERAL
ENVIRONMENTAL EXPLANATIONS

As we have seen, the evidence for an association between demographic variables and language acquisition style is not consistent across studies and tends not to appear in larger-sample studies. Studies could fail to detect those relationships because they examined the wrong point in development (Nelson, 1985) or did not include enough variation in social class (Tomasello & Todd, 1983). On the other hand, any association between gender or birth order and language style may be a small-sample coincidence. Even if we knew that such an association existed, we would not be very much further toward understanding what biases a child toward one strategy or the other. For example, we would not know specifically what about being firstborn is responsible for language style (Bates et al., 1988, p. 59).

Social Explanations

VARIATION IN TYPE OF INPUT

The sheer frequency or preponderance of nouns versus pronouns in parental language is not related to a child's speech style

(Della Corte, Benedict, & Klein, 1983; Furrow & Nelson, 1984). Frequency in parental input is a dubious source of style because no matter how often a child hears something he or she can ignore it if it is not relevant to the messages he or she wants to convey (Bloom et al., 1975, p. 26).

Other authors have argued that acoustic characteristics of the input may be related to the child's strategy. In a case study of a gestalt speaker, the mother talked with great speed and complexity to the boy, with marked intonation contours and repetitions of whole sentences. Perhaps this led to the boy's concentration on holistic attributes of her speech (Peters, 1977, p. 570). However, these surface characteristics are not related in a simple way to features of the child's speech. In a comparison of two children, the mother who spoke fluently but indistinctly had a child with many formulaic utterances, as one might predict. However, unlike Peters's (1977) subject, the mother who tended to exaggerate the prosodic contours of her speech had the child who learned to segment individual words earlier (Plunkett, 1993). Gerken and McIntosh (1993) also found greater pitch contour to facilitate comprehension of function words. Articulatory clarity and emphasis of prosodic contour may have different consequences.

If unclarity of input breeds an "expressive" approach, one would expect the hearing children of deaf parents to lean in a pronominal direction. Surprisingly, three of the five hearing children of deaf parents adopted a nominal strategy (in spoken language), whereas the other two did not appear to adopt either a nominal or pronominal strategy (Shiff, 1976, cited in Bloom & Lahey, 1978, p. 171). Consequently, it does not appear that surface characteristics of the input are completely responsible for children's acquisition style. Perhaps the effects of clarity and prosody depend on the child's style—Hampson and Nelson (1993) suggest that expressive children's language is facilitated by mothers who provide salient and consistent intonation cues.

PARENTAL RESPONSIVENESS VERSUS DIRECTIVENESS

If surface characteristics of the parents' speech are not likely the single causes of the child's style, perhaps other aspects of parent-infant interaction are. Beginning with Nelson (1973), researchers have long suspected that children's language style differences may be related to parents' tendency to be responsive versus directive in social interactions. In general, the more directive mothers had children with less referential vocabularies, whereas maternal feedback on child utterances (both acceptance and rejection) correlated positively with object references (Nelson, 1973). Similarly, Rescorla (1984) found that mothers of early comprehender-referential children were more talkative and provided more descriptions in referential situations such as book reading, whereas the mothers of the less advanced and nonreferential children "tended to proceed through the day with their own activities, often with the TV turned on" (p. 114).[4]

Two potential problems have been raised regarding this maternal responsiveness versus directiveness hypothesis. First, the parents' behavior may be a result of, rather than a cause of, the child's behavior. Second, the conditions under which parents and infants are observed may make them behave in atypical ways. Because these potential problems are not confined to this particular social hypothesis but actually could apply to most similar explanations, they are discussed below in the section entitled "Critique of Social Models."

OBJECT/SOCIAL ORIENTATION OF PARENT-INFANT DYAD

The typical contexts for language socialization may play an important role in children's style of acquisition. Some dyads may focus on objects, whereas others emphasize alternative types of interactions. If children have alternative mechanisms that can take hold in different contexts, perhaps children in dyads that focus on objects emphasize different language learning mechanisms than those who interact primarily in other ways. We do not have to suppose that a highly referential vocabulary results from a *child* who is extremely interested in objects or from a *mother* who frequently labels things. Rather, it could arise because the *dyad* focuses on playing with and talking about objects. Similarly, a social lexicon could result from a *dyadic* focus on participating in activities and using language to coordinate the interaction (Goldfield, 1985-1986, pp. 129-130).

Such a position is supported, to some extent, by indications that mothers of referential and expressive infants differ in their object versus social emphasis. Mothers of referential babies are likely to talk about objects and engage in labeling games, whereas a social focus is more common in mothers of expressive babies (Dore, 1974; Furrow & Nelson, 1984, p. 532).

More pertinent to the hypothesis of *dyadic* object versus social focus are observations that include *both* child and mother influences. Nelson (1973) describes the language development patterns of children whose mothers matched or mismatched them in terms of their orientation to social versus object language. Although matches were facilitative, mismatches could occur, suggesting that the child has some relatively independent preference or bias. Additional evidence of the contributions of *both* mother and child comes from home free-play observations of 45 children at 13 and 20 months. Many aspects of mothers' language at 13 months predicted the child's tendency to produce predominantly nouns at 20 months. Mothers who at 13 months used a lot of nouns themselves, who tended to describe objects, and who used few clichés (e.g., "OK," "There you go") were likely to have referential children at 20 months. Mothers who at 13 months used few nouns and many "performatives" (rhymes, songs, etc.) tended to have expressive children at 20 months. Although maternal factors played a role, several combinations of maternal and child variables *together* were better predictors of child style than either maternal or child variables alone. Twenty-month referential style appeared when the child's 13-month vocabulary emphasized nouns AND when the mother's 13-month conversation emphasized objects (or used nouns) (Hampson, 1989).

Comparable results were obtained in a study of 12 female infants in home play sessions at 12, 15, and 18 months. Children who were high on the dimension of using toys to engage the mother and whose mothers were high on the dimension of talking about toys had the highest proportion of "object-centered words" (labels and descriptions) in the child's vocabulary. Dyads who were low on these dimensions were the lowest and those of mixed characteristics had intermediate values (Goldfield, 1987).

CRITIQUE OF SOCIAL MODELS

As mentioned above, social hypotheses for language development are limited by some methodological problems, such as bidirectionality of influence (who influences whom?) and conditions of observation.

Who Influences Whom?

Lieven's (1978) study of two children and their mothers is frequently cited as demonstrating that parental responsiveness is linked to language acquisition styles. She does say that the referential child's mother responded to 80% of the child's utterances, often with new information or a question that could elicit further talk. In contrast, the expressive child's mother responded to fewer than half of the child's utterances, and those responses frequently ignored the content of the child's utterance, corrected the child's utterance, or were clichés, such as "Really?" or "Oh dear." However, Lieven then had the brilliant idea of analyzing *her own* responses to the children. These paralleled the mothers' responses! Although she may have been imitating the mothers' styles, she says it is hard to respond informatively when the child's utterances are repetitive and not clearly relevant to the ongoing situation—clichés such as "Really?" seem to be the only thing to say (p. 185).

Conditions of Observation

The situations in which we observe parents and infants may affect their interaction. For example, some children may not tend to play with another person while playing with toys. So when we investigators ask these mothers and babies to play with a set of toys in front of our cameras, the parent is almost certain to appear "intrusive." By focusing on toy play, we may be getting an unrepresentative sample of how the infants typically interact. Nontoy play and caregiving episodes might be more characteristic formats for interaction for these dyads (Goldfield, 1987, p. 278).[5]

One study that *did* observe 10 dyads in caretaking contexts still found that mothers of referential children (15 to 19 months old) produced more descriptions and more total utterances, whereas mothers of expressive children were more directive (Della Corte et al., 1983). Although these results are suggestive, it is unclear whether maternal education was also related to child language style in this sample. If so, then we do not know whether maternal speech or maternal education is related to child language style.

Other Problems

Studies of children and their biological parents unavoidably confound genetic and environmental influences. Because parents and children share not only environment but also genes, we do not know which is the source of their similarity (Hardy-Brown, 1983). Measurement issues also pose a problem: Even if environment does play a role, we may never know because maternal style variables are not very reliable and so cannot correlate highly with child variables (Bates et al., 1988). Finally, although one usually expects increases in maternal support to be related to increases in child language ability, one could just as easily expect maternal help when the child is struggling (Bates et al., 1988, p. 238). Bates et al. (1988) conclude that stylistic differences in children's language probably do not originate in linguistic input or social environment. These environmental factors may have an influence, but the initial preference, they believe, comes from the child (p. 240).

Nelson's Cognitive-Social Interactional Model

The hypothesis that language styles result from a *dyadic* object versus social focus seems to be a step in the right direction as it incorporates both child and caregiver contributions. Nelson's

(1985) cognitive-social interactional model elaborates *both* sides of this equation. Nelson believes that individual differences in language appear as the child goes through a transitional phase in cognitive development, and these are influenced by social interaction and by the child's perception of the function of language.

In Nelson's theory, event representations provide the basis for cognitive and language development. By the end of the first year, infants' understanding of the world is organized around familiar events, and language is embedded in these activity contexts. For example, the parent offers another banana to a baby sitting in her high chair: "Do you want more banana?" and the baby holds out her hands. The child probably would not understand those words if she was not in the situation at the time. In the early part of the second year, the child begins to think about the separate components of these familiar events: Different foods appear on the tray at lunch and different words accompany the offer of "more," but if you respond eagerly to the offer you are likely to get it. It is during this unstable transitional time that individual differences are observed. Some children focus on the object realm and use separate words, generally nouns, to isolate the discrete parts of events. Others focus on the social realm, and so language formulas (e.g., "wan' more") are extracted from this particular event and transferred to similar contexts in other events (e.g., "wan' more" piggyback ride) (Nelson, 1985, pp. 122-123).[6]

Why do some children lean toward the social-formulaic approach and others toward the object-noun approach? Nelson (1985) says that it has to do with the child's perception of the function of language as being ideational or interpersonal. This is, in turn, based on an interaction between the child's understanding and the parent's language use. Nelson believes that different contexts have different functions, which lead to speech that differs in both form and function. *Either* exposure to primarily one type of functional context *or* a predisposition to attend to speech in this type of context leads to the child's concluding that language is useful for this type of communication and emphasizing those language forms. Nelson argues that the difference is one of preference rather than competence—most children used all the different functions

(p. 109). A mature understanding of language involves both types of functions and both types of language (p. 115).

Relevant data can be provided on several issues. First, the studies (above) regarding dyadic social versus object focus are relevant to the child's understanding of language functions. Other relevant issues include whether context affects the functions and forms of language that parents and infants use. I also examine the idea that children focus on different aspects of the language they hear around them.

DOES CONTEXT INFLUENCE
WHAT PARENTS SAY TO CHILDREN?

Children and parents experience a number of language contexts, including picture book "reading," play with and without toys, mealtime, and other caregiving events, such as diapering. Some situations may constrain parents to behave more similarly to each other than do other situations. For example, diapering may be a somewhat routine event, with a narrower range of behavior, whereas stylistic preferences of parents may be more evident in play. Two situations that have been of particular interest are book "reading" and play because both may provide different language-learning environments. In the play situation, parents appear to emphasize the variety of interpersonal uses of language, whereas in the book situation, they focus on how language may convey information. Parents are consistent over time in their responses to these different situations (Hoff-Ginsberg, 1991; Jones & Adamson, 1987; Shore et al., 1992; Wiley, Shore, & Dixon, 1989). However, mealtime and play situations may show more parental consistency (Hampson & Nelson, 1993).

DO FORM AND FUNCTION COINCIDE?

There is some supportive evidence that mothers emphasize different parts of the vocabulary when talking to infants in different situations. Mothers talking to 12-month-olds produce a greater frequency and variety of nouns when toys are available than when they are not. Verb frequency and variety are greater in nontoy play when mothers focus more on the activity and interaction. Children with a high percentage of nouns in their early vocabularies had mothers who produced a greater number and variety of nouns during the toy play and who, when toys were *not* available, tended to frequently repeat a small number of nouns (Goldfield, 1993). However, a comparison of two *other* contexts, play and mealtime, showed maternal consistency across situations in use of nouns versus pronouns (Hampson & Nelson, 1993).

It appears that different contexts emphasize different pragmatic functions (interpersonal vs. informational), but it is not as clear that nominal versus pronominal forms follow. For example, "Throw the ball to Mommy" is as effective a command as "Give it here," and the pronominal utterance "What's that?" surely focuses the child on naming.

DO CHILDREN MAKE
DIFFERENTIAL USE OF INPUT?

Nelson argues that children's predispositions to attend to language in certain contexts can influence their conclusions about the basic function of language. If children take an active role in selecting among the speech they hear, one would expect to see no differences between referential and expressive children in the speech they are exposed to, *but* referential children's language would be correlated with different aspects of maternal speech than would expressive children's language.

This was the general pattern of results in two studies of 20-month-olds. Maternal language was measured in a number of different ways, and the mothers of referential and expressive children were very similar, although mothers of expressive children did tend to use fewer nouns and object nouns (Hampson & Nelson, 1993). However, the maternal variables that were correlated with referential children's speech (namely, MLU) differed from those that were related to expressive children's speech (MLU). Among *referential* children, if their mothers used a lot of nouns and discussed objects frequently when the children were 13 months old, the children's MLU at 20 months was high. They had a lower MLU if, at 13 months, their mothers had talked about abstract topics or used many clichés, such as "There you go" (Hampson & Nelson, 1990, 1993). When both mothers and toddlers were examined at 20 months, low-MLU referential children's mothers tended to be directive and asked yes/no questions, and high-MLU referential children's mothers elicited talk with wh- questions (Salkin, 1985). In regard to the *expressive* children, mothers of high-MLU expressive children tended to use a lot of auxiliaries, to use questions that reflected on the child's speech (e.g., "It is small, isn't it?"), and to talk about both objects and people (Salkin, 1985).

It does appear that different children make use of different aspects of the language they hear. This is important as it underscores the idea that language style is a result of an *interaction* between the child's understanding or predisposition and the language to which he or she is exposed.

CRITIQUE OF NELSON'S MODEL

There is much to like in this model. It integrates the literature on individual differences in language development with a broader perspective on early language and cognition. This enriches the individual differences literature by placing it in a meaningful context. It elaborates the early language and cognition literature by pointing out that the task of sorting out the component parts of event representations is complex and that different children evidently tackle it in different ways. Another strength is the centrality it gives to context. So much of children's early language appears to be linked to context that we need to give a high priority to understanding the situations that children are exposed to and how they make sense of them. I hesitate, however, to conclude that the relation between contextual functions and linguistic form is as clear and direct as Nelson implies. I think perhaps the greatest strength of the model is its interactive nature—the balance between the social context and the child's understanding. As Nelson indicates, language style is not simply a matter of the infant copying the language that he or she hears.

Cognitive Internal Explanations

ORIENTATION TO SYMBOLIZATION

Nelson's model identifies language styles as emerging from children taking different approaches to a common task—isolating the component parts of event representations. The orientation to symbolization approach also sees language styles as different emphases within a common task, but the task is described somewhat differently. In using a symbol to communicate with another person, four elements are involved: the self, the other, the symbol (e.g., word), and the referent (the thing the symbol represents) (Werner & Kaplan, 1963). In the model, there are links among these four elements that the child has to come to understand (see Figure 4.1). For example, the links among self, other, and symbol represent the fact that you and I can understand one another by means of this word, and this symbolic communication is part of our relationship. The links among self, symbol, and object represent the idea that I can use this symbol to think about this object, even if the object is not there, and although the symbol reminds me of the object, it is not the same as the object. Understanding all these links is a complex task, and language acquisition styles may be a result of differences between children in what aspects they best grasp.

Words are not the only symbols that the child learns to use. Symbolic play activities, in which one object stands for another (e.g., pretending to lick a block as though it were an ice cream cone), are also thought to involve the same symbol use quadrangle. Perhaps if children employ a similar approach to both of these tasks, we could determine what aspects of symbol use children best understand.

PATTERNERS AND DRAMATISTS

Styles in symbolic development (e.g., patterner vs. dramatist symbolic play) appear to be parallel to language styles. Patterners are described as skilled in fitting objects together to make a pattern. These children are curious—exploring, manipulating, and naming

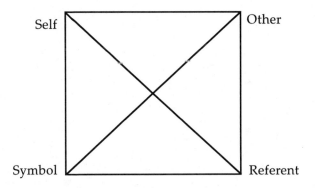

Figure 4.1. The symbol use quadrangle

the object world—and fascinated by how things work. Patterners' language sounds classically referential—heavily biased toward labels and descriptors. In play, they emphasize narration of actual objects and events and indulge in objective comparisons. Dramatists, however, are interested in thoughts, feelings, communication, and relationships and hence sound like ideal examples of expressive speakers who focus on names of people and social and emotional expressions. In play, they use language to engage others in the activity and delight in "embroidering" the situation or narrative (Wolf & Gardner, 1979).

Patterner and dramatist tendencies, like referential and expressive language characteristics, can be treated as dimensions rather than categories. In a study involving factor analyses of data from two samples of 21-month-olds, "dramatism" was evidenced by spontaneous play with realistic props, whereas a "patterner" composite score included protest to object substitutions and play with realistic props following a model. In one of the samples, referential and patterner scores were correlated as were expressive and dramatist scores. In the combined sample, patterner scores were correlated with both language factors but slightly more with the referential factor (Dixon, 1990).

In terms of the symbol use quadrangle, patterners could be said to emphasize the relations among the self, the object, and the symbol and dramatists to emphasize the relations among the self, the other, and the symbol. It is unclear how or why these differences arise—perhaps because of children's overall personalities and characteristic ways of handling information (Shotwell, Wolf, & Gardner, 1979, p. 133).

ANALYTIC AND HOLISTIC
APPROACHES IN SYMBOLIC PLAY

Other researchers have examined the relation between language styles and symbolic play. They have tried to assess the degree to which the child has a grasp of the links among self, referent, and symbol of the symbolic quadrangle, specifically the child's knowledge that the relationship between symbol and referent is *arbitrary*. The word "cow" does not *sound* like a cow—anything can be the symbol as long as we agree on it. A symbolic play task that is thought to draw on this understanding is one involving the substitution of an inappropriate object for one of the props (e.g., a comb is used in place of a spoon) (Shore, Bates, Bretherton, Beeghly, & O'Connell, 1990). One would expect referential children to do well at this task and for it to be related to their language performance. Expressive children, however, might not emphasize this symbol-referent analysis but, rather, the power of the pretense to evoke a familiar activity. Their language might be more closely related to play that uses realistic props to enact a familiar event sequence.

To answer these questions, we (Shore & Bauer, 1983) modeled symbolic play that either did or did not involve an object substitution. For example, a breakfast scene was enacted with a comb as the spoon or with the spoon itself. Referential children (19 to 21 months) showed an increase (over baseline) in pretending in the object-substitution condition, and their utterance length was correlated with their play in this condition. Expressive children showed an increase in pretending following the model with realistic props, and this was the type of pretending that was correlated with their utterance length. These results suggest that referential children's language is more like putting together a set of separate analyzed relations, whereas for the expressive child it is more like reproducing a recognized familiar sequence.

A replication and extension indicated that the processes used in a given symbolic play task depend at least partly on the number, content, and experimental context of the objects (Bauer, 1984, 1985; Dixon & Shore, 1991b; Shore & Bauer, 1984). However, there were consistent relationships between referential children's language and object substitutions in symbolic play and between expressive children's language and symbolic play with realistic objects. Further support for this idea comes from treating language styles as semi-independent continua rather than as dichotomous. Children who imitated the model that included an inappropriate object substitution scored high on a composite referential language factor score (Dixon & Shore, 1991b).[7] These relationships support the idea that referential children prefer an analytic approach and that expressive children prefer a holistic one.

ANALYTIC VERSUS HOLISTIC
APPROACHES IN OTHER ASPECTS
OF SENSORIMOTOR DEVELOPMENT

It seems clear that the symbol use quadrangle involves some type of *analysis,* an ability to distinguish symbol and referent. But it also involves some *rote* or holistic processes as well. Because the relationship between symbol and referent is arbitrary, the child has to be able to obtain this link by imitation and just memorize it. For example, "cow" means *cow*—no reason, it just does. Finally, to put these relations into practice, the child has to *intend to communicate* his or her meaning to the other. Individual differences could result from the child differentially emphasizing analytic versus rote processes (Bates, 1979). We have seen how these processes may be evident in symbolic play. Perhaps other sensorimotor tasks as well can show us analytic and rote/holistic processing and their relationships (if any) to language style. For example, tool use (e.g., a stick to rake in a toy) has been proposed as a task that requires children to analyze means to achieve ends and so is analogous to analyzing symbols as means to achieve communicative ends (Bates, 1979).

A study of two children learning Danish showed that these children's language style was related in an interesting way to their tool use. The expressive child began using frozen phrases as social-communicative means well before he applied means-ends to tool use, whereas the referential child showed tool use prior to acquiring vocabulary (Plunkett, 1985, pp. 108-109). Bauer (1985) also found that correlations between language measures and operational causality and means-ends were in opposite directions for expressive and referential subsamples.

ANALYTIC VERSUS HOLISTIC PROCESSING

There is some support, then, for the idea that language styles involve some ability to analyze the relationships among words and the world and another ability to reproduce a whole, packaged event or link. The analytic versus holistic processing idea appears not only in terms of Werner and Kaplan's (1963) symbol use quadrangle but in other ways as well. A number of researchers suggest that linguistic styles result from relative emphasis on analytic versus holistic information processing strategies (e.g., Peters, 1977).[8]

Snow and Bates (cited in Bates et al., 1988) have described different versions of the analytic-holistic distinction. One interpretation is in terms of *content versus frequency.* Referential children would be said to be stronger at detecting informative elements, such as content words, whereas expressive children would be said to be better at picking up high-frequency elements, such as formulaic phrases. A different description uses *comprehension/analysis for understanding versus production/analysis for reproduction.* One could describe referential children as "interested in . . . what people are trying to say," whereas expressive children are "production-driven," "trying to sound like other people" (p. 65). Future work needs to explore and clarify these different interpretations of what we mean by analytic versus holistic processes.

CRITIQUE OF COGNITIVE INTERNAL MODELS

I think the weakness of this type of research is in finding ways to tap into *how* babies are processing information. The predominant methodology has been correlational: Children who do well on aspects of language that we think were probably extracted by means of analytic processes are also likely to do well on tasks that we think also rely on analytic skills. There are many ways in which this research can go wrong. We might be wrong in the way we have conceptualized how children extract that particular aspect of language. We might be wrong in what skills the other tasks require. Perhaps these tasks do not have abilities in common with language, or even if they do, task-specific skills may overwhelm any relationship with language. Then there are all the usual problems of whether or not the babies were motivated to do their best and whether or not the measures are reliable. Although correlational research has its limitations, we cannot look inside the child's head to see just exactly how he or she is processing linguistic information. Using a variety of tasks and examining their relationships does help us make some inferences about common processes.

Internal Explanations

TENDENCY TO IMITATE

Some views identify "imitativeness as a central dimension of individual differences" (Goldfield & Snow, 1989, p. 310). Imitativeness may be used to account for children's acquisition of formulaic phrases early on, their production of high-frequency items, such as pronouns, and their "messier" phonological systems. However, this is controversial because the task type and the presumed level of the child's understanding may influence the tendency to imitate and thus obscure the relationship, if any, with linguistic style.

Children do differ considerably in their tendency to imitate. In Bloom, Hood, and Lightbown's (1974) classic study, "Allison" never imitated more than 6% of the utterance types she used, whereas "Peter" imitated at least 27%—and both were remarkably consistent across time in their tendency to imitate. Imitativeness tended to be associated with expressive/pivot-open style. However, differences can appear between expressive speakers in their level of imitation (Ferguson & Farwell, 1975, p. 421).

Two studies report a paradoxical result of greater imitation of *object names* among expressive children (Bates et al., 1988; Nelson, 1973). This suggests that these children imitate nouns but do not incorporate them into their vocabularies (Nelson, 1973). By contrast, other researchers have found an association between referentiality and imitation of object names, especially novel ones (Leonard, Schwartz, Folger, Newhoff, & Wilcox, 1979; Nelson et al., 1985; Starr, 1975).

CRITIQUE OF IMITATIVENESS

In sum, we have some studies that show an expressive advantage for imitation, and others that show referential children more likely to imitate. Yet others indicate that imitativeness is unrelated to either of these (Bretherton et al., 1983; Shore, 1986).

Perhaps the differences between children may not be how MUCH they imitate but WHAT they imitate (Goldfield & Snow, 1989) or perhaps WHEN or WHY (Bloom et al., 1974, p. 410). Language style differences may affect the *reasons* why children imitate—as evidence of understanding or just to keep the conversation going (Bates et al., 1988, p. 45). Language style may also affect whether children imitate what they *do* understand or what they *do not* (Goldfield & Snow, 1989, p. 307). Perhaps referential-nominal children filter imitations through their current rule system—they do not imitate things that they cannot produce spontaneously, whereas expressive children do (Bates et al., 1988, p. 48). Another possibility is that high levels of imitation occur at *both* low and high levels of understanding. It appears that imitativeness probably does not define language style (Bates et al., 1988, p. 134).

OBJECT/PERSONAL ORIENTATION
AND MASTERY MOTIVATION

If we characterize language styles as object oriented versus socially oriented rather than analytic-holistic, it is tempting to think that language styles will be related to social versus object mastery motivation (e.g., Wachs, 1993). Social mastery motivation is typically evidenced by obtaining and retaining others' attention. Object mastery motivation is assessed by the child's efforts to produce an effect with an object or to solve problems involving objects.

There is some support for drawing such comparisons. Referential children have been described as interested in exploratory, pretend, and problem-solving play with toys, whereas less referential children were more socially oriented and their toy play was described as more varied but more conventional (Rescorla, 1984, p. 109; Rosenblatt, 1977). Little evidential detail is given in either of these studies for these conclusions.

However, there are some problems with linking language style and mastery motivation. One is that the locus of object interest is not in the child but in the dyad. Perhaps it is not the sheer amount of toy play or social interaction but, rather, episodes of *shared* interaction around objects that contribute to the acquisition of referential language. In fact, in one study, the referential child spent *less* time in toy play and exploration than did the 11 other children in the study, including the most highly expressive child (Goldfield, 1985-1986). In further work with this sample, there was *no* relationship between a social versus object play composite score and the contents of the children's vocabularies (Goldfield, 1987). Instead, children who acquired many nominal words often used objects to engage their mothers' attention. Expressive children were just as interested in objects and people as referential children but tended not to overlap these two domains, preferring to do one or the other (Goldfield, 1985-1986, p. 130). Similarly, although Maia's language (see Chapter 2) was clearly expressive, she interacted in complex and sustained ways with both people and objects, and her first words were used both for reference and for regulating social exchanges (Adamson et al., 1984).

Another problem is that difficulties in measurement have foiled at least one attempt to find a relationship between language and mastery motivation. This research involved two samples of 29 children. Referential and expressive multiword speech composite scores were created using a factor analysis. Factor analyses were also used to construct composite scores for mastery motivation. In the combined sample, object mastery included how frequently children performed goal-directed behaviors and how long they would keep trying to solve a problem after a model demonstrated a solution. Social mastery included social initiatives with and without objects (e.g., looking and vocalizing to an adult; and showing or handing an object to an adult). *Neither* of these mastery motivation scores was related to language style scores. The most likely reason is that the measures of mastery motivation were unstable because different tasks were used in the two different samples. These task differences may have affected the type of mastery motivation the children showed. The results cast doubt on a simple mapping of mastery motivation to language style (Dixon, 1990).

TEMPERAMENT

Because language is so involved with social relationships and cognition, it is tempting to believe that language style differences may relate to common ways of approaching the physical and social worlds (Goldfield, 1985-1986). At least three different temperamental variables have been suggested to underlie individual differences in language: boldness versus timidity, activity level and attention focus, and sociability.

Boldness Versus Timidity

When individual differences in language are described in terms such as cautious/conservative versus bold/risk taking (e.g., Horgan, 1981), it is intriguing to note the similarity to temperamental variables such as shyness/vigilance versus outgoing/bold (as in

Kagan, Reznick, Clarke, Snidman, & Garcia-Coll, 1984). Referential children are likely to be described as outgoing and interested in novelty, whereas expressive children are more likely to be described as cautious, conservative, or self-conscious (Fillmore, 1979, pp. 224, 226; Goldfield, 1985-1986, p. 130; Macken, 1978, p. 228).

Paradoxically, it is not always clear whether the expressive or the referential child should be characterized as risk taking. The expressive child could be construed as taking risks because he or she seems to learn whole forms and worry later about analyzing them. However, more morphological overgeneralization has been seen in nominal children, so they could be seen as "not afraid to make a mistake" (Bates et al., 1988, p. 60).

Attention Level and Activity

Concentration, attention span, and frustration tolerance are predictive of more sophisticated comprehension and production in 2-year-olds (Slomkowski, Nelson, Dunn, & Plomin, 1992). Similarly, children with more stable emotionality and neutral affect tend to learn words faster (Bloom, 1993, p. 182). Early comprehender-referential children have been found to enjoy quiet, focused activities as early as 12 months, whereas same-age children with lower comprehension were "fidgety, inattentive and bored" when the mother attempted to engage them in play with books or toys and were "constantly on-the-go, stubborn, and difficult to handle" (Rescorla, 1984, p. 105). Dixon and Shore (1993) also found that children who had high duration of orientation scores at 13 months scored high on a referential factor score at 20 months.

Sociability

Toddlers' outgoingness/extroversion is predictive of more sophisticated language comprehension and production, not only at the time of measurement (age 2 years) but into the future (ages 3 and 7) (Slomkowski et al., 1992). Sociability has been related to expressive language style variables in 28-month-olds. These correlations were modest, and partial correlations indicated that sociability was not the reason for the relationship of these language variables to each other. The researchers conclude that temperament does not *cause* individual differences in language development, but a highly sociable temperament could facilitate reliance on a more rote/holistic strategy (Bates et al., 1988). Previous work with this sample (Bretherton, et al., 1983) indicated that the temperament measures were related to *observed* language measures (rather than interview), suggesting that transient situational factors may have been responsible for the association.

CRITIQUE OF INTERNAL MOTIVATION
AND TEMPERAMENT MODELS

Many of the concerns regarding the cognitive internal models also apply here, such as difficulties in assessing internal motivation and temperament. Temperament and mastery motivation may be so broad as behavioral dispositions that their overlap with language style is difficult to detect, especially in the small samples that are typical of this research. I think it is probably more likely (or at least easier to detect) that two areas, such as language and symbolic play, share *specific* skills, such as symbol-referent analysis.

Perhaps most important, language style is itself a complex phenomenon that has been described in different terms, such as referential versus expressive, analytic versus holistic, and risk taking versus conservative. As was seen in Chapter 3, probably the best-documented characterization is in terms of analytic versus holistic processes. These *form* variables (e.g., preponderance of nouns and pronouns) are the types of variables that have been used in large-scale correlational studies of the relationship between language style and mastery motivation or temperament. However, it would make much more sense to look for relationships between language style and mastery motivation if *functional* aspects of language were used (e.g., relative emphasis on informational vs. interpersonal purposes). Similarly, it would make a lot more sense to look for relationships between language style and temperament by using language variables that related to, for example, risk taking (e.g., tendency to imitate familiar vs. novel words).

Consequently, although the current case for mastery motivation and temperament as sources of language style looks unpromising, I think we have to do as the British juries do and bring in a verdict of "not proven."

Language-Specific Internal Explanations

BIOLOGICAL/GENETIC UNDERPINNINGS FOR LANGUAGE STYLES

It is possible that there is a biological basis, perhaps genetic, for individual differences in language specifically as opposed to indirectly via temperament or cognition. This may relate to the other language-specific and neurological explanations discussed below.

The possibility that individual differences in language development have a genetic basis is often overlooked. One reason for this is that genetic underpinnings are confused with theories of an innate universal language acquisition device (LAD). However, genetic factors could be responsible for differences between individuals as well as commonalities (Goad & Ingram, 1987, p. 420; Hardy-Brown, 1983, p. 612; Locke, 1988, p. 667). Although to my knowledge there are no behavior genetics studies that attempt to disentangle genetic versus environmental contributions to language style, variability in *rate* of communicative development (see Hardy-Brown, 1983; Thompson & Plomin, 1988) and syntactic sophistication (Munsinger & Douglass, 1976) have been related to genetic factors.

A study by Leonard, Newhoff, and Masalem (1980) of the phonological development of identical twins who were raised together yields some interesting thoughts about genes and environment as sources of individual differences. The twins typically slept and played in the same room and received caregiving together. Whatever was said to one twin was generally heard by the other. Insofar as it was possible to determine, these children had "essentially the same linguistic input" (p. 14), and of course their genetic makeup was identical. Although their phonological development was quite similar, there were differences in consonants used by the children and the order/time of emergence of consonants. The twins also differed in how consistently/variably they produced particular sounds. This is striking, as it would seem that this is the ideal situation—the same genes, the "same" environment—for demonstrating uniformity of development. Yet individual differences appear nonetheless. Leonard et al. (1980) argue that different children will derive different hypotheses in the process of actively constructing phonology (p. 26).

Explanations Involving
the Language System

Some explanations for language styles have to do with development within the language system itself. These take different forms:

1. Different language processes (comprehension and production) are dissociated from each other (this hypothesis is discussed in Chapter 2 under "Comprehension").
2. Different aspects of the language system (e.g., semantics and syntax) are distinct or develop out-of-synchrony.
3. Within an aspect of language (e.g., syntax), different portions are differentially sensitive to environmental input.

DISSOCIATIONS BETWEEN ASPECTS OF LANGUAGE

Frequently, individual differences in language are attributed to a discrepancy between semantics/pragmatics and syntax. For example, one holistic child was thought to adopt this strategy because he was older and more conversationally experienced and thus perhaps grasped the social purpose of some forms without the necessary syntactic competence to analyze them and consequently proceeded with unanalyzed forms (Richards, 1990, p. 220).

A similar type of semantic versus syntactic type of difference is found in content words versus function words because content words carry most of the idea of what the sentence is about and function words show the grammatical relations (Gleitman, 1988). These also tend to map linguistic style: Nominal-analytic children tend to excel at content words, whereas the utterances of pronominal-holistic children contain more function words. Consequently, perhaps linguistic style arises from a disjunction between semantics and syntax.

If semantics and syntax form two separate systems, one would expect children's early lexical-semantic development to be unrelated to their later syntactic development (beyond effects of overall rate of development). On the contrary, Bates et al. (1988) found a strand of lexical-analytic-conceptual variables that could be traced from first words to early productive grammar, independent of overall development. This suggests, instead, that these two aspects of language flow together in development.

DIFFERENTIAL SENSITIVITY TO LANGUAGE INPUT

Gleitman and colleagues distinguish between "environmentally insensitive" and "environmentally sensitive" aspects of language. The former are "universal properties of natural languages" (Gleitman, 1988, p. 169), which are thought to result from maturation of biologically based language-processing abilities and therefore be less influenced by caregiver input.[9] Environmentally sensitive elements would be ones that differ across languages and so presumably are more influenced by differences in caregiver input. Gleitman indicates that the use of closed-class morphology is one example of an aspect of language that is closely tied to input variation.

In their discussion of this hypothesis, Bates et al. (1988) argue that one could extend this distinction to apply to individual differences between children. According to such an account, "nominal children are sticking primarily to the exercise of innate linguistic hypotheses; pronominal children are relying on some kind of general-purpose learning device" (p. 62). They go on to say that for this explanation to work one would have to have some independent criterion for saying that some aspect of grammar will or will not be environmentally sensitive.

A similar idea was explored by Cazden (1966) when she hypothesized that universal aspects of language, such as expressing basic grammatical relations, may be less susceptible to environmental influences and show fewer individual differences than language-unique aspects. This view would have difficulty accounting for research by Bloom and Ramer regarding differences in the emergence of basic grammatical relations (see Chapter 2).

NEUROLOGICAL EXPLANATIONS

One possibility for explaining language acquisition styles, mentioned by a number of researchers in this area, is the left-right brain hemisphere distinction. To generalize, the left hemisphere seems to be specialized for sequential/analytic type processing, whereas the right seems to specialize in simultaneous/holistic processing. Though the left is usually said to be more important for language, the right plays some role in intonation and formulaic speech (Gazzaniga, 1983; Zaidel, 1983). Consequently, it is tempting to associate pronominal-expressive style, given its emphasis on wholes, prosody, and formulaic speech, with the right hemisphere and to associate nominal-referential speech with the left hemisphere (Bates et al., 1988, p. 63). If that were the case, one would expect that right hemisphere damage (or developmental delay) would lead to referential style, whereas left hemisphere damage (or developmental delay) would result in expressive style.

Alternatively, one might hypothesize differences *within* the left hemisphere. Each hemisphere has anterior (near the front of the head) and posterior (near the back of the head) regions. Left *posterior* damage in adults is associated with Wernicke's aphasia (fluent nonsensical speech, with apparently impaired comprehension). Therefore, one might predict such damage (or developmental delay) to result in expressive style acquisition. In contrast, left *anterior* damage in adults is associated with Broca's aphasia (halting telegraphic production with relatively unimpaired comprehension). Consequently, one could expect damage (or developmental delay) in this area to result in referential style of acquisition.

Neither the left versus right hemispheric hypothesis *nor* the anterior-posterior hypothesis receives clear support from research on childhood aphasia. In particular, Wernicke's aphasia is not often seen in children, even in cases of left posterior damage (Bishop, 1988). One study of the early language development of five children with brain injuries even reports a trend in the oppposite direction: Children with left *posterior* injuries tended to produce fewer closed-class morphemes (i.e., telegraphic utterances). The counterintuitive conclusion is that the left posterior region may support holistic style in early acquisition (Thal et al., 1991).

An alternative "local details" hypothesis is proposed to account for these data, by analogy to the data on brain damage and visual spatial tasks. Children and adults with left hemisphere (particularly left *posterior*) damage show difficulties in extracting local details in visual-spatial tasks (e.g., when asked to draw a house, they leave out parts such as windows and chimney). In contrast, children and adults with right hemisphere damage show problems with overall configuration (e.g., drawing parts such as windows and chimney but not in appropriate relation to one another). Perhaps the left posterior region mediates the extraction of local details, and expressive children produce unanalyzed elaborate phrases complete with function words precisely because they excel at this detailed level of production. In other words, we have been misled by the term "holistic" into ignoring the local details that these children in fact produce (Bates, Thal, & Janowsky, 1992; Thal et al., 1991). One could view their inclusions of function words and inflections as a detailed reproduction of the stimuli they hear (Goldfield & Snow, 1989, p. 311). However, the "local details" hypothesis does not account for the unintelligibility often associated with the expressive-holistic style—one would think they wouldn't be so "mushmouthed." On the other hand, poor articulation abilities might interfere with producing details that are in fact distinguished.

CRITIQUE OF LANGUAGE-
SPECIFIC INTERNAL HYPOTHESES

Athough it is possible that there are language-specific biological underpinnings to individual differences in language, I think most of the hypotheses of this type have not, so far, been very informative.

In the future, behavior genetics studies could be of considerable value in helping us unconfound genetic and environmental influences. Such work could, in principle, inform us whether the differences observed in parental language are or are not related to differences in their children's language style. Such work could provide clear demonstrations of how different characteristics of children interact with different rearing environments to yield different patterns of behavior. But we cannot stop with an estimate of the heritability of individual differences in language. Just saying that children's language development differs because their genes differ would not tell us much—we would need to know more about the mechanisms. Genes could have a part in almost any of the explanations we have considered—from cognitive processes, to temperament, to differential rate of maturation of brain areas. Because their influence is potentially so ubiquitous, just saying "It's due to genetic differences" without specifying how those genetic differences relate to behavior would not be very informative. Similarly, we learn very little from the statement that children differ in their language development because of different possibilities available in the hypothetical innate LAD. This explanation appears merely to rename the problem—children differ in their language development because in principle language development can differ. This would provide only an illusion of explanation—we attribute differences to genetic or innate factors when we do not know what else to attribute them to (Dent & Zukow, 1990).

Why Do Children Differ in Their Approach to Language Acquisition?

Our understanding of the causes of individual differences in language is necessarily limited by the nature of the phenomenon. Language is inherently interactive, and so bidirectionality of influence makes causality very difficult to determine. Similarly, we cannot randomly assign infants to different rearing conditions, and our opportunities to take advantage of "natural experiments" that would unconfound genetic and environmental influences are limited. The correlational methodologies that we generally have to employ are very vulnerable to the small samples that provide the majority of evidence we have. There are other methodological reasons to be very cautious in drawing conclusions about the factors that contribute to language styles, such as difficulties in defining and measuring our constructs in ways that will be unobtrusive and representative of typical behavior.

With those limitations in mind, however, some explanations seem more plausible or more useful than others. The general environmental (demographics) account seems too vague to be useful. At the other end of the spectrum, the language-specific biological hypotheses have so far also not been very informative. It appears to be fairly clear that parental language *forms* are not copied directly into children's language styles. The social influence hypotheses suffer from the methodological problems discussed by Hardy-Brown and Bates et al. Of the social hypotheses, a dyadic or interactional account, such as Goldfield's or Nelson's, is the most plausible as such a complex acquisition is likely to have multiple causal influences.

At this point, not enough is known about the mastery motivation and temperament hypotheses to evaluate them usefully. My hunch is that they are *too* broad and that they do not give enough role to the interaction with the task, context, and environment. Although there may be some children who are "object people" and others who are "people people," it probably depends on situation, task, and point of view. Labeling objects might be a very socially engaged and engaging activity (Bates et al., 1988, p. 52).

A useful component of an explanation would be some term at an intermediate level of generality, such as analytic versus holistic processes or attention to detail. Such a term could have a biological basis or not, but it would provide a bridge between language performance as an outcome and the broad underlying causes of nature or nurture. Such a term could also be useful in showing the appropriate links between language and certain other cognitive tasks, such as symbolic play.

Of course, all these explanations are not mutually exclusive. In fact, there are several good reasons why multiple factors could play a role:

1. *Bidirectionality of influence.* Children and their families influence each other. A cognitive bias (or temperamental quality or social preference, etc.) on the part of the child is quite likely to interact with parental interests and style of expression.
2. *Language is a complex system.* Different explanations might apply to different aspects of the developing language system—imitativeness, for example, may turn out to be particularly important in accounting for phonological development, whereas parental responsiveness might be particularly important for pragmatic development. In addition, as previously mentioned, languages differ in their analytic versus holistic structure and consequently may emphasize different learning mechanisms.
3. *There may be different language style dimensions.* Although we know most about analytic versus holistic dimensions, there may be social versus object orientations and risk taking versus conservative dimensions that are semiseparable and have different causal underpinnings.
4. *Timing.* It is also possible that the relative importance of different causal factors (e.g., genetic vs. environmental influences) might differ over time. Genes turn on and off with development, and children are exposed to different environments with age (Hardy-Brown, 1983). Bates's (1979) theory of language development emphasizes how different component processes for language emerge at different times and so require different types of cognitive support.

As in a multiple-choice test, the answer may very well turn out to be "all of the above."

Notes

1. Studies finding girls referential and boys expressive are Bates et al. (1988) (Julia), Bloom et al. (1975), Dore (1974), Peters (1977), Plunkett (1985), Ramer (1976), Stoel-Gammon and Cooper (1984), and Vihman (1981). Studies finding the opposite trend or no gender effects are Adamson, Tomasello, and Benbisty (1984), Bates et al. (1988), Bates et al. (1994), Bauer (1984, 1985), Clark (1974), Goldfield (1985-1986,

1987), Goldfield and Reznick (1990), Horgan (1980) (Kelly), Huxley (1970), Lieven (1978), and Macken (1978).

2. Studies finding firstborns referential and later-borns expressive are Bates et al. (1988) (Julia), Goldfield (1985-1986), Goldfield and Resnick (1990), Lieven (1978), Nelson (1973), and Nelson et al. (1985). Studies finding opposite trends or no birth-order effects are Bates et al. (1988), Bates et al. (1994), Bauer (1984, 1985), Bloom (1993), Bloom et al. (1975), Pine and Lieven (1990), Plunkett (1985), and Tomasello and Todd (1983).

3. Several authors have noted similarities of noun lovers and noun leavers to Bernstein's (1970) "restricted" (concrete and context dependent) and "elaborated" (abstract and less context dependent) codes in different SES groups. However, Bernstein may have confounded social class with familiarity of setting and conversational partners (Ellis & Beattie, 1986, p. 99).

4. The *type* of parental response to the child may relate to the child's strategy. Mothers who frequently imitated their child's utterances at 22 months often had imitative-referential children 5 months later (Nelson et al., 1985, p. 452).

5. Furthermore, the *type* of toys available (e.g., enactment vs. manipulative) may influence how mothers talk, such as variety of sentence types, and frequency of questions (Bloom, 1993).

6. Bloom (1970) makes a similar argument: that nominal versus pronominal style differences in early grammar are a result of differences in the way that children make links between their knowledge of the world and linguistic structures (p. 233). These may be as important as (if not more than) the frequency or complexity of grammatical structures in the language they hear. Because children's life experiences are different, their language acquisition will also be different (p. 227).

7. In 12- to 16-month-olds, one would probably expect nouns to relate to "naming gestures" (e.g., putting a toy telephone receiver to an ear) and social phrases to gesture routines (e.g., waving "bye-bye"). These expectations were disconfirmed by Bates et al. (1989). Perhaps infants tend to have *either* a gesture or a word for an object or activity (Bates, 1979), so that infants with many object words would not necessarily have many naming gestures.

8. A related idea is that language styles reflect differences in field independence/dependence, with the nominal-referential style being associated with field independence and the expressive style being associated with field dependence. Bates et al. (1988) do not find this explanation satisfactory because field independence-dependence is a single continuum, and they find two (or more) language style dimensions (p. 64).

9. A similar argument is made regarding phonological development: "The child is born with a highly constrained language acquisition device which limits what a possible human language is" (Goad & Ingram, 1987, p. 420). Very limited variability in phonological development may be possible as a result of options allowed by the language acquisition device.

5

Conclusions
and Future Directions

In this chapter, I attempt to find out where we are and where we are going in our journey toward understanding individual differences in language development and their implications for how children acquire language. I first describe the present position, summarizing the complex research findings reviewed so far. I also make an agenda for future explorations. Some of those roads not yet traveled relate to some current trends in developmental theory and how they might apply to individual differences in language development. Finally, I consider how individual differences might deepen our understanding of language development.

Where Are We?

If this book were a novel, it would be a long and complicated story, with multiple characters and a plot full of twists and flashbacks. Now, like the author of a mystery story, I will have the detective come in at the end to try to pull all the loose ends together and show how they make a coherent case to present to you, the jury.

SUMMARY OF LANGUAGE STYLE DIFFERENCES

It appears that children show referential versus expressive characteristics very early in their language learning career, that referential style in production is related to a similar bias in comprehension, and that referential children use words for objects in a context-flexible way.

Children may differ considerably in how they go about acquiring both word order rules and grammatical morphemes. These different strategic approaches manifest themselves in a variety of ways (e.g., nominal vs. pronominal content, early frozen vs. later analyzed acquisition of grammatical morphemes, and pivot-open vs. telegraphic grammars). It seems clear that all children do not learn syntax in the same way.

Children's phonological development does not show a common, characteristic pattern. Furthermore, phonological development does not appear to be isolated from other aspects of development, such as grammatical strategy or lexical development. Children who take a formulaic syntactic approach often focus on the "tune" rather than the "notes." Some add new sounds cautiously, whereas others appear to proceed in a more diverse way. In either case, the sounds that children produce are linked to the words they are learning, so phonological development is not autonomous.

Children do apparently differ in their use of language as a communicative medium and the pragmatic purposes for which they tend to use it. However, it is not clear how these differences relate to stylistic dimensions in other aspects of language, such as vocabulary.

ARE THERE STYLES OF LANGUAGE DEVELOPMENT?

Styles of individual differences have their own distinctive qualities, are generalized patterns of behavior, persist over time, and are independent of general developmental level. We can describe at least two different language styles in ways that show their unique qualities. At present, the best-documented contrast is between analytic and holistic themes. Reasonably good evidence links early lexical/vocabulary development with early grammatical development, indicating both coherence across tasks and across time. Neither style necessarily has an advantage in terms of vocabulary development or utterance complexity. With development, it appears that *both* styles tend to incorporate elements of the other rather than one catching up with the other. Finally, it appears that referential style is not simply a result of greater intelligence or more rapid development.

WHY DO CHILDREN DIFFER IN THEIR APPROACH TO LANGUAGE ACQUISITION?

Such a complex acquisition is likely to have multiple causal influences. A promising explanation is some cognitive tendency, such as analytic versus holistic processes or attention to detail. This cognitive bias may or may not have a biological basis and is likely to interact with parental interests and style. There are several reasons why multiple factors could play a role: Different explanations might apply to different aspects of the developing language system or to different dimensions of language styles. Finally, the relative importance of different causal factors might differ over time.

Where Do We Go From Here?

RESEARCH ON THE NATURE OF INDIVIDUAL DIFFERENCES IN LANGUAGE

Because of the small samples used, the differences between children's language have been generally described in terms of a contrast between individuals or small groups of children. However, we can think of these as dimensions common to all children's development. To understand the nature and number of these dimensions, we need to know more about how developments in different aspects of language (semantic, syntactic, phonological, and pragmatic) relate to one another.

As we obtain more information about the different aspects of language, our definition of language styles may change. One trend in the recent literature is a tendency to move away from common nouns as the single measure of style (e.g., Bates et al., 1994; Pine, 1992). One candidate for a redefinition of styles involves the relative pace of comprehension and production. Children who say more than they apparently understand may be relying on rote/holistic processes, whereas those whose comprehension matches or exceeds production presumably use more analysis (Bates et al., 1994). Much more information is needed about developmental changes and stylistic differences in comprehension.

When we obtain more data about how individual differences in phonological and pragmatic development relate to lexical and grammatical development we may find that two "styles" are not enough to describe the variations we see. It is possible, for example, that the risk taking versus conservative dimension is a separate issue from whether the child concentrates on analysis or holistic processing or that the social versus object orientation may take the place of "referentiality" as we discover more about how children use language in context.

GENERALIZABILITY ACROSS CULTURES AND LANGUAGES

The literature reviewed thus far typically involves normally developing children, acquiring English, and mostly within a middle socioeconomic status. Several investigators have pointed out cultural or subcultural variation in what aspects of language are valued and in how families expect children to learn language. Different cultural expectations for language participation by infants may foster different strategies for isolating sounds, words, and phrases from the ongoing speech stream than the "baby talk" addressed to infants by middle-class European American mothers (Lieven et al., 1992, p. 306; Peters, 1983). For example, in the African American community of Trackton, infants listen to the flow of conversation all around them, and their early utterances often consist of imitations of ends of phrases and sentences they overhear (Heath, 1983, p. 91).

The structure of different languages has implications for the areas in which one might expect stylistic differences. For example, in Italian, pronouns are less common in everyday speech and so are not as likely to be associated with a rote-imitative cluster as they are in English (Bates et al., 1988, pp. 274-275). Similarly, in Mandarin Chinese, grammatical morphology (frequently associated with an expressive-holistic style) is rare, and noun-noun combinations (frequently associated with a referential-analytic style) hardly ever appear in children's speech (Erbaugh, 1982). One wonders whether anything like the strategies observed in English also occur in Chinese or other similar languages (Bates et al., 1988, p. 275).

SOURCES OF INDIVIDUAL DIFFERENCES IN LANGUAGE

Research on a broad variety of fronts may help further our understanding of the origins of individual differences in language.

Behavior genetics approaches can be used to separate genetic from environmental sources of variance (Hardy-Brown, 1983). Once such broad distinctions have been made, it will be useful to explore more specific mechanisms and to explore gene-environment interactions (e.g., people responding differently to children of differing genetic predispositions).

One possibility that has not yet received much investigation is that expressive children may have more rote phrases because they literally hear the input better prior to analysis or may have particularly good acoustic memory buffers, whereas referential children may have superior attention capabilities (Bates & MacWhinney, 1987, pp. 188-189). We also need more information to evaluate the mastery motivation and temperament hypotheses.

A variety of relevant data can be gathered on social-cognitive contributors to language styles: whether dyadic focus on social versus object interaction is relevant to the child's interpretation of the function of language, whether the child makes differential use of the available language, and whether context influences the type of language used. Task and context can have profound effects on performance, which means we must exercise caution in saying that some ability is "in the child" or even "in the dyad." Consequently, we need to examine more than one interactive context before drawing conclusions about the typical kind of dyadic interchange (Goldfield, 1987). To examine Nelson's idea that children's understanding of the functions of language drives their acquisition of language forms, more work that examines the relationship between vocabulary and its use in context is needed.

Many questions arise about the relationship between language differences and cognitive development. A valuable contribution would be research on how language style differences relate to how children make links between their knowledge of the world and linguistic structures. Further work is also needed on the proposal from Bates (1979) that individual differences appear when there is an imbalance among cognitive underpinnings for language: analytic (means-ends), gestalt (imitation), and communicative intent.

Snow and Bates (cited in Bates et al., 1988) have raised the possibility that referential children may be stronger at detecting informative elements, such as content words, whereas expressive children may be better at picking up high-frequency elements, such as formulaic phrases. This could be linked to the "local details" hypothesis (see Chapter 4) (Bates et al., 1992). Other work could also be aimed at exploring the conditions that support children's extraction and use of formulaic speech. For example, we could benefit from experimentation on children's perceptions of the units of language, evidence on how chunks of language can be dissected and recombined, and cross-linguistic evidence on the role of large recurrent chunks (Peters, 1983, pp. 95-96).

RESEARCH ON LATER INDIVIDUAL DIFFERENCES

We are not sure whether the child's early preference will be evident in later language-using tasks, such as referential communication. There is some evidence that stylistic differences in relative use and elaboration of verbs and nouns may exist in the grade school years, based on analyses of children's spontaneous stories (Hass & Wepman, 1974). Even if stylistic variation is a phenomenon restricted to acquisition tasks, it might resurface when the person is faced with a new language-learning task.

A distinction between cautious/conservative versus error-prone/risk taking has been also used to describe second-language learners. Some second-language learners are rule-oriented—their utterances can easily be described within a set of rules and they tend to move in a clear-cut fashion from one stage to the next. Others are "data gatherers" whose systems are less easily characterized by a set of rules (Hatch, 1974). Similarly, a distinction has been made between gestalt and rule modes of second-language learning (Krashen & Scarcella, 1978).

A similar risk taking versus conservative contrast has been observed in children learning to read. Some children skipped around on workbook pages, previewed text, and approximated or skipped over unknown words. Others worked carefully and methodically, recalled details of stories in sequence, and focused on faithfully translating written words into speech, rarely skipping, slurring, or guessing words (Bussis, Chittenden, Amarel, & Klausner, 1985). One can only wonder whether these second-language learning and reading styles are consistent with the children's early approach to spoken language (Peters, 1977, p. 571).

IMPLICATIONS FOR INTERVENTION

Goldfield and Snow (1989) point out that knowing there are many ways to learn a language "should help us to think more creatively about therapy, intervention and education" (p. 321). Not all children will benefit equally from the same classroom or therapeutic activities, and if one approach does not work, another might.

The findings of formulaic approaches to second language (see Chapter 3) might be applied to bilingual education. School-aged children learning English as a second language focus on using language to communicate with others while actively striving to construct the rules of the new language. They need support in learning how to *use* the new language and opportunities for social interaction rather than drills (Hudelson, 1990).

We can also speculate about applications to language disorders. Sometimes, pathology is seen as occupying the extremes of normal variation. It might be that some child language disorders represent the extremes of the analytic and holistic dimensions described in normal children. Some children with language delays may evidence extremes of telegraphic speech (Bates et al., 1988, p. 276) or overreliance on unanalyzed forms (Richards, 1990, p. 233). Bloom et al. (1975) suggest that the limited lexical representation seen in some language-disabled children might result from an inability to shift from a system with constant pronominal forms to a system with grammatical categories. The echolalia (pathological degree of imitation) of autistic children and the "cocktail party syndrome" (contentless chatter) seen in some hydrocephalic children with low IQs may be seen as two candidates for extreme versions of the imitative-pronominal-rote approach (Bates et al., 1988, p. 276).

Researchers in dyslexia have also distinguished between holistic-versus segment-based processes in "dysphonetic" versus "dyseidetic" early readers. Dysphonetic children have considerable difficulty "sounding out" words—making use of the individual letters of the words. By contrast, dyseidetic children have difficulties with remembering words and letters as a *whole* (Fried, Tanguay, Boder, Doubleday, & Greensite, 1981). One wonders whether these difficulties with written language are related to the child's approach to acquiring spoken language.

New Directions in Language Development Theories and Their Relationship to Individual Differences

Several new lines of thought are beginning to have an impact on developmental theorizing. Ecological psychology stimulates new thinking about the organism and environment as a system, a new angle from which to describe the environment and the functional bases of language acquisition. Nonlinear dynamic systems theory ("chaos" theory) provides a captivating way of visualizing and quantifying concepts such as stability and transition and the recurrent but ever changing patterns, parallels, and analogies seen in cognitive and language development. Parallel distributed processing or connectionist models in cognitive psychology hold promise as metaphors for emergent properties and transitional states.

Ecological Theory

Ecological psychology derives from James Gibson's (1979) work in perception. When applied to language acquisition, this theory says that neither the child nor the environment alone is responsible for language acquisition but, rather, "the functioning of perceptual systems that detect language-world relationships and use them to guide attention and action" (Dent, 1990a, p. 679). Dent (1990a) says that these perceptual systems enable children to detect invariant (unchanging, constant) relations between language and the world. In the theory, these perceptual systems make memories and mental representations unnecessary.

Dent contrasts this perspective with the traditional cognitive explanation, such as the symbol use quadrangle I reviewed in Chapter 4. In this type of view, spoken language is thought of as a sort of "code" in which arbitrary symbols are related to objects and events in the world. The child's memory for events involving the symbol and the referent helps create the mental link between the two. Dent, however, objects to the "code" metaphor for language. She says that ecological theory "explains how experience in itself is meaningful without the addition of associated memories or innate ideas" (p. 680).

Dent (1990b) objects to nativist theories for the same reasons, namely, the rejection of mental representations. She says that ecological approaches do not involve inner mental codes, which are "either 'triggered' by experience . . . or built up out of categorized experience . . . and which have to be related to relevant aspects of the world" (p. 759).

In terms of its account of individual differences, I imagine that the predictions from this theory would not differ significantly from social or social interactional explanations. They might also examine how acoustic characteristics of the input relate to grammatical segmentation. Emphasis would be placed on the child's detection of environmental invariants, and to the extent that the environment differs significantly, individual differences would also be anticipated in the child's language.

Chaos Theory

Nonlinear dynamic systems theory (a new perspective in physical and biological sciences) is full of phrases that are tantalizing for developmental psychologists: for example, "sensitive dependence on initial conditions," "points of instability," "discontinuity," "phase transition," and "qualitative shifts." A complete description is beyond the scope of this book, but there are several aspects of this approach that are of potential interest for developmental psycholinguists studying individual differences.

NONLINEAR INFLUENCES ON SYSTEMS

Linear systems are ones in which you can assign a constant influence to one of the factors—the more the merrier. Linear systems can also involve the combination of factors—the importance of one of the factors depends on one or more others, as in an ANOVA interaction. Nonlinear ones, however, are those in which the importance of one factor depends on something else, which in turn depends on the first. Gleick (1988) uses some apt metaphors to describe such systems: "The act of playing the game has a way of changing the rules, . . . like walking through a maze whose walls rearrange themselves with each step you take" (p. 24).

Even simple physical systems, such as the motion of a hockey puck, often involve nonlinear terms. Surely, then, developing psychological systems must do so also because they involve bidirectionality of influence between caregiver and child. Language development is likely to involve nonlinearity.

EQUILIBRIUM, STABILITY, AND IDEAL END STATES

Before chaos theory, physical and biological sciences tended to ignore the messiness of nonlinear systems. The same could be said to be true of psychologists, like Piaget, who were much more interested in the elegance of the universals of development, in which Piaget felt that the real mechanisms of development were to be found, rather than in the messy details of individual differences. It could also be said to be true of Chomsky, who is interested in modeling the idealized linguistic *competence* of an idealized speaker rather than in error-pocked *performance* spoken by real people in day-to-day conversations.

Although chaotic systems can end up in a static end point, it is much more typical that they show themes and variations, never quite escaping a pattern but never quite repeating themselves. We can think of language in the same way. There is no one pure adult language that children are acquiring; rather, there is a set of individual speakers' versions of a language. You can go a long distance specifying what all English speakers have in common, but ultimately the elements of the language system are unique to an individual, *and* that individual changes over time.

RESPONDING TO MULTIPLE INFLUENCES: EMERGENT CAUSES FOR PATTERNS OF CHANGE

When we say that a behavior is *emergent* or is an *emergent property*, we mean that it results from the confluence of many factors or component processes, none of which dictates the pattern or form of the behavior. An example used by Bates (1979) is Tinbergen's description of the zigzag "dance" of the stickleback fish. This complex behavior is not a result of innate instructions that tell the fish to go this way and then turn that way. Rather, it arises from the push and pull of opposing approach and avoidance motivations. In chaos theory terms, these different motivations would be called "stable attractors."

Chaotic systems often show complex patterns of behavior when two or more attractors are simultaneously operating. Individual differences can give us clues to the potential influences that are operating on a system (Thelen, 1990, 1992). An application of this idea in language development is to think of analytic and gestalt processes as two stable attractors that together pull on children's processing of utterances. Styles of language acquisition could possibly be seen as emerging depending on the relative strength of these two attractors.

In development, the component processes or attractors could change over time. Thelen (1990, 1992) argues that behavior emerges because of the cooperation of many subsystems in the context of a particular task. In her view, new behavioral forms can arise as emergent properties when component processes change and create instability. This sounds very similar to Bates and her colleagues' (1979) arguments about component processes for language development and to the changing relationship between gesture/symbolic play development and language (Shore et al., 1990). The relative strength and/or developmental timing of these component processes could set the stage for individual differences in language development.

SENSITIVE DEPENDENCE ON INITIAL CONDITIONS

We have always assumed that "given an *approximate* knowledge of a system's initial conditions and an understanding of natural law, one can calculate the *approximate* behavior of the system" (Gleick, 1988, p. 15). However, because of "sensitive dependence on initial conditions," this assumption may be gravely in error. Edward Lorenz (as described by Gleick, 1988) discovered that small differences in the initial values of variables used in making a computer model of the weather could compound until the two output weather patterns looked completely different. Long-range prediction becomes impossible because one cannot isolate a system from its context, one can never know or measure completely exactly all the influences upon it, and approximately the same input will *not* give approximately the same result.

Sensitive dependence on initial conditions relates to the nature-nurture question. It recalls the Leonard et al. (1980) study of the identical twins (see Chapter 4). These children had, as best as we can tell, the same genes and the same environment. But although their phonological acquisition was similar, it was not the same. Small differences add up and can create substantial differences in outcome. Similarly, Bloom (1970) says, "The differences among [the children's language] must reflect the importance of individual differences in the interaction between cognitive function and experience, *which could not be assumed to be the same for any two children*" (p. 227, emphasis added).

Sensitive dependence on initial conditions may mean that we are in error in framing the nature-nurture question as "What must be in the genes in order to make use of the environment?" When arbitrarily small differences in context render long-range prediction impossible, it may not be useful to take an *idealized* version of language, subtract from it the information available in a *generalized* environment, and attribute the rest to nature.

Parallel-Distributed Processing (PDP) or Connectionism

Connectionism is another metaphor that is "in the air" these days in discussions of cognitive and linguistic development. Plunkett and Sinha (1992) provide a very good discussion of the relevance of connectionist models for language acquisition. Connectionist systems are interesting for several reasons. They suggest ways in which language processing might take place without internalized symbols and rules. They show flexibility and resilience in ways that some people believe is more like human thinking than are traditional artificial intelligence approaches (Bechtel & Abrahamsen, 1991, pp. 17, 56-65).[1]

WHAT ARE CONNECTIONIST NETWORKS?

A commonly discussed type of PDP system contains an input layer of units that encodes information about stimulus input, an output layer that gives specifications about the response, and one or more "hidden" layers. Typically, the system is initially set so that the weights on the interconnections are random—information is sent from one unit to any other units in the next layer in a random fashion. Although there are different learning procedures, the most typical ones are essentially a trial-and-error learning process. A stimulus is presented, a random response is given, and then the operator tells the system what the correct answer should have been. The system then adjusts the weights on the connections to reduce the discrepancy between the response that it gave and the one it should have given. Over many trials, eventually the system comes to give the desired responses. One can examine the progress of the system during training to see whether the patterns of responses show intermediate levels of understanding or error patterns that are typical of human acquisition (Bechtel & Abrahamsen, 1991).

Information is represented in the network in a distributed fashion in the form of the pattern of weights on the various connections. Usually the activations of hidden units do not have a simple obvious correspondence to features of the input. For example, in learning a family tree, there may not be a single unit that is "on" for all female family members and "off" for males (i.e., "symbolizes" gender). Consequently, these distributed encodings are not "symbols" in the usual sense. The lack of symbols and rules makes connectionist architecture radically different from traditional artificial intelligence approaches.

LANGUAGE DEVELOPMENT WITHOUT SYMBOLS?

We have long assumed that what children learn over the course of language development is how to manipulate symbols by means of rules. It could be argued that describing language acquisition in terms of symbols almost necessitates nativism: "Since the operations performed by the system all involve manipulating symbols, it seems that at least some symbols and initial ways to manipulate symbols must be innate" (Bechtel & Abrahamsen, 1991, p. 104). In contrast, a connectionist system is quite dependent on the nature and sequencing of the input it receives as well as on the initial architecture of the system. These systems have been used to illustrate how rulelike behavior can emerge even when no "innate" information was previously provided to the system about how to develop such rules.

Connectionism challenges the assumption that in order to deal with external symbols one needs an internal symbol system. Connectionists argue that although linguistic theory describes language as symbol combinations perhaps children do not have to. Instead of internalizing these external symbols, children may use pattern recognition to process them (Bechtel & Abrahamsen, 1991, p. 249). Pattern recognition processes allow a system to recognize similar (but different) examples of the same thing (e.g., the number "2" in different handwriting). One could think of the basic subject-verb-object ordering in English as a pattern that you come to recognize in varying appearances. Such processes need not involve internal symbols.

Connectionists have illustrated the applicability of their ideas to language development in simulations of the acquisition of past-tense verbs. Although this procedure is controversial, it has been used to simulate the stagelike emergence of intermediate solutions and the emergence of organized behavior without the explicit statement of rules (McClelland, 1989; Plunkett & Sinha, 1992).

HOW DOES CONNECTIONISM
ACCOUNT FOR INDIVIDUAL DIFFERENCES?

As in any other developing system, the initial architecture as well as the environment of instances to which the system is exposed will influence the system's functioning. Therefore, the potential exists for individual differences, based either on differences in input or on differences in initial settings. However, currently, connectionists do not appear to have addressed the problem of individual differences in how the system(s) process information.

One might ask whether the basic structure and functioning of connectionist systems are more suitable for modeling the processes typical of some individuals than the processes of others. Here, one can only speculate. It could be argued that the system sounds like a "referential" learner in that comprehension apparently precedes production (Bates et al., 1988). Learning at first proceeds so gradually that it is not evident in overt performance (McClelland, 1989, p. 36). On one hand, the search for categories, patterns in the input, and stagelike progressions sounds like the stereotypical referential approach. On the other hand, more expressive characteristics are learning by the frequencies of input patterns that are treated as wholes and learning by risking outputs that are then correctable (W. E. Dixon, personal communication, June 1993). Perhaps a connectionist model is an analogy for expressive processing, whereas the traditional symbolic approach models the more rule-bound referential processing.

In any case, a connectionist approach might shed light on some of the controversies surrounding the reasons for individual differences in language development. As long as one conceptualizes language development as consisting of developing symbols and rules, then individual differences depend on whether or not you have certain symbols or rules. This issue becomes less problematic if we set aside internalized rules as the achievement of language development. If we instead characterize language development as a pattern recognition problem, children could differ in the size of linguistic patterns they pick up on, as suggested by Peters (1983). Such a process could be context sensitive. As one will recall, Nelson proposed that habitual contexts lead to different forms of language. Progress in understanding contexts might also help us understand the cases in which children are expressive in some situations and referential in others.

Common Themes in Ecological, Chaos, and Connectionist Theories and How They Apply to Individual Differences

A common theme across several of these approaches is that *mental symbols are out and context enmeshment is in.* A major point of similarity is an emphasis on the fit between organism and environment and the enmeshment of cognitive processing with the real world of activity with people and objects (Bechtel & Abrahamsen, 1991, p. 26). A complete discussion of the pros and cons of mental symbols is well beyond the scope of this book. I think, however, that the cognitive constructivist approaches (e.g., orientation to symbolization explanations in Chapter 4) and the social interactionist approaches would completely agree about the importance of context in the emergence of early language and cognition, although most would argue that mental representations are essential to language.[2]

In fact, in Nelson's approach it is context that enables the child to *attend to correlational structure of the input*, which is a second common theme. Ecological and connectionist approaches are centered on pattern recognition, which involves figuring out what features tend to go together. This process may relate to Nelson's and Bloom's arguments that individual differences could result from children attending to *different* correlations between words and the world.

The ubiquitousness and power of relatively simple processes such as pattern recognition lead these theorists to *question domain specificity*. For example, "language is not a distinct type of knowledge or 'organ of the mind' " (Dent, 1990a, p. 690). The connectionists leave this issue open, but they do emphasize how the same type of processing can be applied to a variety of different problems. As we have seen, individual differences in language cross the semantic-syntactic domain border, may have links to phonological and pragmatic development, and may also be related to processes outside of language.

Another common theme is that *self-correcting systems resist breakdown*. Connectionist models and chaotic systems show graceful degradation and self-correction. Such flexibility in the face of disruption may be very advantageous for biological systems (Libchaber, cited in Gleick, 1988, p. 194). It may also account for how a relatively stable language development "style" could also show variations with context.

Finally, all these approaches have in common a tendency to use *emergent causality* as an explanation. They tend to think of behavior as emerging at the interface of multiple probabalistic influences. Such a context-embedded explanation seems likely for individual differences in language.

What Can Individual Differences Tell Us About the Mechanisms of Language Development?

We are interested in individual differences in language development because we believe that the way something develops may give us clues about its underlying nature or about the mechanisms that make it possible. For example, universality tempts one to think of innate factors, although other explanations are also possible. But what about individual differences? Some modularity theorists suggest that individual differences might be useful in detecting mental abilities that are distinct from other aspects of cognitive functioning and that are part of a uniquely human biological heritage (e.g., Gardner, 1983; Gross, 1985). Although cognitive constructivists and social interactionists challenge both domain specificity and nativism, they also look to individual differences in language development for clues to alternative theories about how language develops. However, we need to be cautious in our interpretations—the things that cause individual differences do not necessarily cause universals.

McCall (1981) and Hardy-Brown (1983) suggest that we ought to be cautious about the linkage between individual differences and mechanisms of development. These are, in principle, separate issues. To make this point, McCall uses the example of the redwood tree (see Chapter 1). In Hardy-Brown's terms, the causes of differences *between* groups or species are not necessarily the same as the causes of differences *within* groups. Consequently, it is a mistake to argue that evidence for an environmental or genetic cause for individual differences in language implies that the same factor is responsible for universals of language.

It seems to me that we have two different types of questions here. One type asks "What contributes to children's tendency to rely more heavily on one or another ability/component in language acquisition, and is this the same thing that makes language development itself possible?" The other type asks "From the different patterns of development, can we deduce abilities/components that can be used by different children to crack the code of language?"

In regard to the first question, the factors that contribute to average differences over time may not be the same as those that contribute to making individuals different from one another. Generally, we think of explaining behavior using the framework of additive linear combinations in an analysis of variance. That is, a certain number of the points in your score are due to factor A, other points due to factor B, and still other points due to their interaction, and finally we add some points for "error." In the ANOVA we are interested in the factors that cause mean differences, say, between the average performances at two different ages—not the "error" of individual differences.

But this way of thinking may miss some important considerations. Any individual's score comprises the factors that cause group differences AND those that cause individual differences. It is an *assumption* that these compound in a linear way. These developmental and stylistic factors might react (in a chemical sense) in surprising ways. If we think of organism-environment interaction as a *transaction* (i.e., a matter of *reciprocal* influence) rather than a linear interaction, the combination may be less predictable. Consequently, even though the sources for universals and individual differences in language development may be different, we may not be able to ignore the impact of stylistic factors in gaining an understanding of factors that affect developmental universals.

In regard to the second question, I think that individual differences *can* tell us something about the functioning of a system. We will miss something fundamental if all we look at is an idealized mean that characterizes everyone as a group and no one as an individual. From the point of view of chaos theory, individual differences stop being the error term in the analysis of variance. Deviations from an idealized mean become the key to understanding the workings of the system rather than inconvenient numerical dust to be swept under the rug (Thelen, 1990). It is not just in the universals of development that developmental mechanisms are to be found. Lewontin has criticized developmental biologists for being "so fascinated with how an egg turns into a chicken that they have ignored the critical fact that every egg turns into a different chicken and that each chicken's right side is different in an unpredictable way from its left" (cited in Oyama, 1985, p. 121). Although the factors that cause differences between individuals are not necessarily those that cause universals, modularity theorists as well as cognitive constructivists and social interactionists suggest that individual differences can give us information about how language develops.

Theoretical Implications: Modularity Theories and Nativism

If all children are born with an innate Language Acquisition Device that contains syntactic information that they will need to become competent users of their native language, two predictions generally (although not necessarily) follow:

1. All children will acquire language essentially the same way, according to the same maturationally determined timetable (Klein, 1978, pp. 9-11).
2. Language acquisition, particularly syntactic acquisition, will be domain specific, unrelated to developments in other areas, such as cognition.

I think there is reason to question both of these statements.

IMPLICATIONS FOR UNIVERSALITY

It seems fairly clear that the standard "one word to telegraphic" speech progression of language development just is not the case for some children. We have to build theories that allow this type of variation, as it evidently occurs. We should be aware of the possibility of a developmental sequence opposite to the one we have traditionally been led to look for. A formulaic developmental

sequence would be one "starting with unanalyzed chunks, proceeding through a stage of more or less complete analysis, and
returning to refused but analyzed chunks" (Peters, 1983, p. 91).
Most children will exhibit aspects of both formulaic and analytical
use, and a balanced account of language development cannot
focus exclusively on the analytical "word to sentence" progression
(Nelson, 1985, p. 108; Peters, 1983).

IMPLICATIONS FOR DOMAIN SPECIFICITY

Is syntax related to other aspects of language? The evidence for
stylistic connection between early vocabulary acquisition and
early sentences indicates a certain degree of coherence between
the child's approach to semantics (i.e., vocabulary) and syntax.
Children who begin by acquiring a large number of frozen phrases
have a different task facing them in acquiring productive control
over grammar than do children who start off with primarily single
words. The links between semantics and grammar may appear for
several reasons, but they all violate Gardner and Fodor's criteria
for modules, in particular, "that they be separate processors which
do not rely on each other's output and separate developmental
histories" (Bates et al., 1988, p. 280).[3, 4]

Is language related to the rest of cognition? The relationships
that have been observed between children's approach to language
and their performance on sensorimotor cognition tasks (e.g., tool
use) suggest links between language and other cognitive functions. Similarly, the consistent relationship between language
style and symbolic play supports the idea that a common element
such as symbol-referent analysis is involved (Dixon & Shore,
1991b; Shore & Bauer, 1984). These studies also make it clear that
the number, content, and experimental context of the objects affect
how children approach these tasks. However, the little extant
research on mastery motivation does not indicate a simple link
between preference for people versus objects and language style.
Consequently, we cannot say that one's approach to language is
linked to a *pervasive* approach to thinking and interacting. More
likely, different aspects of the child's approach to language have

similarities to specific cognitive abilities at particular points in time (Bates, O'Connell, & Shore, 1987).

Toward an Alternative Theory

If the individual differences observed in language are not congruent with a modularity/nativist account of language development, do those differences provide suggestions for an alternative theory? They do, largely because the variability observed between children does not appear to be random. Rather, there appear to be a small number of fairly consistently observed ways to go about the task of learning to use language. For example, children showing a clear stylistic preference suggests that other children may also be employing the same mechanism, although perhaps to a less extreme degree (Goldfield & Snow, 1989, p. 320). Nelson's theory and the "orientation to symbolization" approach emphasize the idea that styles are relative emphases that children take within a common task. In other words, by seeing what children can specialize in, we may learn what the components are.

Nominal-analytic skills and pronominal-holistic skills seem to be available to some degree in all children. One advantage of thinking in terms of two dimensions is that both are positive characteristics. Another advantage is that this image fits with results of large-scale correlational studies, with the convergence-of-style phenomenon, and with observations that stylistic variations are sensitive to context.

Analytic and holistic dimensions have to do with how children make sense of the linguistic forms in utterances heard and relate these to the objects and events around them and have implications for the forms that children acquire. In addition, children may grasp the informational or interpersonal functions of language—or both. Children who prefer informational functions may have strengths in analytical processing and extract nominal forms, while interpersonal functions may link to holistic processes and pronominal forms. But this link may depend in part on the relationship between forms and functions in the language he or she hears.

We need more information about parents' and children's uses of different forms to accomplish different functions in different contexts to see how these functional dimensions relate to ones that have more to do with forms.

Finally, other stylistic differences, which may or may not be related, have to do with a speed-accuracy trade-off in acquisition. For example, children's approaches to category learning and their strategies for phonological acquisition have been described in bold-scattered versus conservative-systematic terms (e.g., Rescorla, 1984). These may also turn out to be best described as two semi-independent dimensions in which all combinations are possible, including some children making rapid systematic advances and others slow scattered efforts.

In examining individual differences in language we have learned that both analytic and holistic processes, as ways of coping with language input, are likely to be common across children and that children's grasp of language functions is likely to support their efforts to make sense of whatever size units they work with. In other words, there are probably both social and cognitive components of language acquisition. We need to be aware of the dynamic interplay between the language a child hears and his or her efforts to make sense of it. A child's stylistic bias may lead him or her to make different use of parental utterances than another child would. Research on maternal input to language acquisition should not ignore differences between children in their interest in or sensitivity to that input (Hampson & Nelson, 1993).

We have also learned how important context is in children's early acquisition. Context plays an important role in many of the nonnativist approaches to individual differences in language. Context embeddedness may support simple but powerful mechanisms that can be applied to a variety of tasks, including language learning. Context embeddedness also leads us to rethink our framing of the nature-nurture question. We cannot think of "nature's" contribution as being whatever is not available in a generalized version of "nurture" because small differences in context can have cumulative small effects that can add up to big differences in outcome.

Consequently, a theory of language development should attend to the multifaceted nature of this accomplishment and the varying ways that children make their way into becoming language users. This transition is one of the most important developmental passages we make—becoming a language user transforms all our subsequent cognitive and social development. Individual differences are most salient at times when the system is undergoing transitions (McCall, Eichorn & Hogarty, 1977; Nelson, 1981; Thelen, 1990, 1992). The individual differences observed in this major transition to language use are most likely a result of the complex interaction of factors in the child, in the environment, and in the language being learned. Consequently, individual differences in language development provide us with a particularly good example of the "complexities of developmental interaction" and a window on the "creative constructive dynamic of development" (Nelson, 1981, p. 183).

Notes

1. Even though these are frequently called "neural networks," there are several important ways they differ from how the brain works (Hinton, 1989).

2. According to the decontextualization hypothesis, children's early words and symbolic play gestures are tied to specific situations and objects and gradually become more flexible (e.g., Bates, 1979; Nelson, 1985; Werner & Kaplan, 1963; Wertsch & Stone, 1985). Bechtel and Abrahamsen (1991) describe relationships between this idea and connectionism.

3. Bates et al. go on to say that a modular separation between grammar and semantics may appear later, either as a late-maturing innate mechanism for processing more complex grammar or as a learned, practiced module for automatic processing of grammar.

4. Phonology, like syntax, has been claimed to be an aspect of language development that is relatively autonomous, isolated from other aspects of development, largely biologically based, and under maturational control (e.g., Gardner, 1983, p. 80). This view is questionable, for reasons described in Chapter 2.

References

Adamson, L. B., Tomasello, M., & Benbisty, L. L. (April, 1984). *An "expressive" infant's communication development*. Paper presented at the International Conference on Infant Studies, New York.

Anastasi, A. (1958). Heredity, environment, and the question "How?" *Psychological Review, 65*, 197-208.

Bates, E. (1979). *The emergence of symbols*. New York: Academic Press.

Bates, E., Bretherton, I., & Snyder, L. (1988). *From first words to grammar: Individual differences and dissociable mechanisms*. New York: Academic Press.

Bates, E., & MacWhinney, B. (1987). Competition, variation and language learning. In B. MacWhinney (Ed.), *Mechanisms of language acquisition* (pp. 157-193). Hillsdale, NJ: Lawrence Erlbaum.

Bates, E., Marchman, V., Thal, D., Fenson, L., Dale, P., Reznick, J. S., Reilly, J., & Hartung, J. (1994). Developmental and stylistic variation in the composition of early vocabulary. *Journal of Child Language, 21*, 85-123.

Bates, E., O'Connell, B., & Shore, C. (1987). Language and communication in infancy. In J. D. Osofsky (Ed.), *Personality processes: Handbook of infant development* (2nd ed., pp. 149-203). New York: John Wiley.

Bates, E., Thal, D., & Janowsky, J. S. (1992). Early language development and its neural correlates. In I. Rapin & S. Segalowitz (Eds.), *Handbook of neuropsychology* (Vol. 7, pp. 69-110). Amsterdam: Elsevier.

Bates, E., Thal, D., Whitesell, K., Fenson, L., & Oakes, L. (1989). Integrating language and gesture in infancy. *Developmental psychology, 25*, 1004-1019.

Bauer, P. J. (1984). *Referential and expressive language styles: A comparison in non-linguistic domains*. Unpublished master's thesis, Miami University, Oxford, OH.

Bauer, P. (1985). *Referential and expressive styles in linguistic and non-linguistic domains: A longitudinal examination*. Unpublished doctoral dissertation, Miami University, Oxford, OH.

Bechtel, W., & Abrahamsen, A. (1991). *Connectionism and the mind*. Padstow, Cornwall, UK: T. J. Press, Ltd.

Bellugi, U. (1971). Simplification in children's language. In R. Huxley & E. Ingram (Eds.), *Language acquisition: Models and methods* (pp. 95-120). London: Academic Press.

Bernstein, B. (1970). A sociolinguistic approach to socialization: With some reference to educability. In F. Williams (Ed.), *Language and poverty* (pp. 25-61). Chicago: Markham.

Bishop, D. (1988). Language development after focal brain damage. In D. Bishop & K. Mogford (Eds.), *Language development in exceptional circumstances* (pp. 203-219). Edinburgh: Churchill Livingstone.

Bloom, L. (1970). *Language development.* Cambridge: MIT Press.

Bloom, L. (1973). *One word at a time.* The Hague: Mouton.

Bloom, L. (1993). *The transition from infancy to language: Acquiring the power of expression.* Cambridge, UK: Cambridge University Press.

Bloom, L., Hood, L., & Lightbown, P. (1974). Imitation in language development: If, when and why? *Cognitive Psychology, 6,* 380-420.

Bloom, L., & Lahey, M. (1978). *Language development and language disorders.* New York: John Wiley.

Bloom, L., Lightbown, P., & Hood, L. (1975). Structure and variation in child language. *Monographs of the Society for Research in Child Development, 40*(2, Serial No. 160), 1-78.

Bowerman, M. (1976). Semantic factors in the acquisition of rules for word use and sentence construction. In D. Morehead & A. Morehead (Eds.), *Directions in normal and deficient child language* (pp. 99-180). Baltimore: University Park Press.

Braine, M. D. S. (1976). Children's first word combinations. *Monographs of the Society for Research in Child Development, 41*(1, Serial No. 164), 1-96

Branigan, G. (1976). Sequences of single words as structured units. *Papers and Reports on Child Language Development, 12,* 60-70. (Eric Document Reproduction Service No. ED 162 510)

Bretherton, I., McNew, S., Snyder, L., & Bates, E. (1983). Individual differences at 20 months: Analytic and holistic strategies in language acquisition. *Journal of Child Language, 10,* 293-320.

Brown, R. (1968). The development of wh-questions in child speech. *Journal of Verbal Learning and Verbal Behavior, 7,* 279-290.

Brown, R., Cazden, C., & Bellugi-Klima, U. (1969). The child's grammar from I to III. In J. P. Hill (Ed.), *Minnesota symposia on child psychology (1967)* (Vol. 2). Minneapolis: University of Minnesota Press. (Reprinted in A. Bar-Adon & W. F. Leopold (Eds.), *Child language: A book of readings* (pp. 382-412). Englewood Cliffs, NJ: Prentice Hall, 1971)

Bruner, J. (1983). *Child's talk: Learning to use language.* New York: Norton.

Bussis, A. M., Chittenden, E. A., Amarel, M., & Klausner, E. (1985). *Inquiry into meaning: An investigation of learning to read.* Hillsdale, NJ: Lawrence Erlbaum.

Cazden, C. B. (1966). On individual differences in language competence and performance. *Journal of Special Education, 1,* 135-150.

Chomsky, N. (1968). *Language and mind.* New York: Harcourt, Brace & World.

Clark, R. (1974). Performing without competence. *Journal of Child Language, 1,* 1-10.

Clark, R. (1977). What's the use of imitation? *Journal of Child Language, 4,* 341-358.

Della Corte, M., Benedict, H., & Klein, D. (1983). The relationship of pragmatic dimensions of mothers' speech to the referential-expressive distinction. *Journal of Child Language, 10,* 35-44.

Dent, C. H. (1990a). An ecological approach to language development: An alternative functionalism. *Developmental Psychobiology, 23,* 679-703.

Dent, C. H. (1990b). Language, thought, and other mutualities of organism and environment: A reply to Oyama's commentary. *Developmental Psychobiology, 23,* 759-760.

Dent, C. H., & Zukow, P. G. (1990). The idea of innateness: Effects on language and communication research. *Developmental Psychobiology, 23,* 551-555.

Dixon, W. E., Jr. (1990). *Individual differences in three domains of cognitive development.* Unpublished doctoral dissertation, Miami University, Oxford, OH.

Dixon, W. E., Jr., & Shore, C. (1991a, April). *A confirmatory factor analysis of language style.* Paper presented at the biennial meeting of the Society for Research in Child Development, Seattle.

Dixon, W. E., Jr., & Shore, C. (1991b). Measuring symbolic play style in infancy: A methodological approach. *Journal of Genetic Psychology, 152,* 191-205.

Dixon, W. E., Jr., & Shore, C. (1992, May). *Confirming linguistic styles.* Paper presented at the International Conference on Infant Studies, Miami Beach, FL.

Dixon, W. E., Jr., & Shore, C. (1993, March). *Short term stability and temperamental predictors of linguistic style.* Paper presented at the biennial meeting of the Society for Research in Child Development, New Orleans.

Dore, J. (1974). A pragmatic description of early language development. *Journal of Psycholinguistic Research, 4,* 423-430.

Ellis, A., & Beattie, G. (1986). *The psychology of language and communication.* New York: Guilford.

Erbaugh, M. (1982). *The acquisition of Mandarin Chinese.* Unpublished doctoral dissertation, University of California, Berkeley.

Ferguson, C. A. (1979). Phonology as an individual access system: Some data from language acquisition. In C. J. Fillmore, D. Kempler, & W. S.-Y. Wang (Eds.), *Individual differences in language ability and language behavior* (pp. 189-202). New York: Academic Press.

Ferguson, C., & Farwell, C. (1975). Words and sounds in early language acquisition. *Language, 51,* 419-439.

Fillmore, L. W. (1979). Individual differences in second language acquisition. In C. Fillmore, D. Kempler, & W. S.-Y. Wang (Eds.), *Individual differences in language ability and language behavior* (pp. 203-228). New York: Academic Press.

Fodor, J. A. (1983). *Modularity of mind.* Cambridge, MA, and London: MIT Press.

Fodor, J. (1985). Precis of "The modularity of mind." *Behavioral and Brain Sciences, 8,* 1-42.

Fried, I., Tanguay, P., Boder, E., Doubleday, C., & Greensite, M. (1981). Developmental dyslexia: Electrophysiological evidence of clinical subgroups. *Brain and Language, 12,* 14-22.

Furrow, D. (1980). *Social and asocial uses of language in young children.* Unpublished doctoral dissertation, Yale University.

Furrow, D., & Nelson, K. (1984). Environmental correlates of individual differences in language acquisition. *Journal of Child Language, 11,* 523-534.

Gardner, H. (1983). *Frames of mind.* New York: Basic Books.

Gardner, H. (1985). The centrality of modules. *Behavioral and Brain Sciences, 8,* 12-14.

Gazzaniga, M. S. (1983). Right hemisphere language following brain bisection: A 20-year perspective. *American Psychologist, 38,* 525-537.

Gerken, L., & McIntosh, B. J. (1993). Interplay of function morphemes and prosody in early language. *Developmental Psychology, 29(3),* 448-457.

Gibson, J. J. (1979). *The ecological approach to visual perception.* Boston: Houghton Mifflin.

Gleick, J. (1988). *Chaos: Making a new science.* New York: Penguin.

Gleitman, L. R. (1988). Biological dispositions to learn language. In M. B. Franklin & S. S. Barten (Eds.), *Child language: A reader* (pp. 158-175). New York: Oxford University Press. (Originally published in W. W. Demopolous & A. Marras (Eds.), *Language learning and concept acquisition* (pp. 3-28). Norwood, NJ: Ablex, 1986)

Goad, H., & Ingram, D. (1987). Individual variation and its relevance to a theory of phonological acquisition. *Journal of Child Language, 14,* 419-432.

Golden, M., & Birns, B. (1976). Social class and infant intelligence. In M. Lewis (Ed.), *Origins of intelligence: Infancy and early childhood* (pp. 299-352). New York: Plenum.

Goldfield, B. (1985-1986). Referential and expressive language: A study of two mother-child dyads. *First Language, 6,* 119-131.

Goldfield, B. A. (1987). The contributions of child and caregiver to referential and expressive language. *Applied Psycholinguistics, 8,* 267-280.

Goldfield, B. (1993). Noun bias in maternal speech to one-year-olds. *Journal of Child Language, 20,* 85-99.

Goldfield, B. A., & Reznick, J. S. (1990). Early lexical acquisition: Rate, content, and the vocabulary spurt. *Journal of Child Language, 17,* 171-183.

Goldfield, B., & Snow, C. (1989). Individual differences in language acquisition. In J. Berko Gleason (Ed.), *The development of language* (2nd ed., pp. 303-325). Columbus, OH: Merrill.

Gross, C. G. (1985). On Gall's reputation and some recent "new phrenology." *Behavioral and Brain Sciences, 8,* 16-18.

Hampson, J. (1988). Individual differences in style of language acquisition in relation to social networks. In S. Salzinger, J. Antrobus, & M. Hammer (Eds.), *Social networks of children, adolescents, and college students* (pp. 37-58). Hillsdale, NJ: Lawrence Erlbaum.

Hampson, J. (1989, April). *Elements of style: Maternal and child contributions to expressive and referential styles of language acquisition.* Paper presented at the biennial meeting of the Society for Research in Child Development, Kansas City, MO.

Hampson, J., & Nelson, K. (1990). Early relations between mother talk and language development: Masked and unmasked. *Papers and Reports on Child Language, 29,* 78-85. (Eric Document Reproduction Service No. ED 338 050)

Hampson, J., & Nelson, K. (1993). The relation of maternal langauge to variation in rate and style of language acquisition. *Journal of Child Language, 20,* 313-342.

Hardy-Brown, K. (1983). Universals and individual differences: Disentangling two approaches to the study of language acquisition. *Developmental Psychology, 19,* 610-624.

Hass, W. A., & Wepman, J. M. (1974). Dimensions of individual difference in the spoken syntax of school children. *Journal of Speech and Hearing Research, 17,* 455-469.

Hatch, E. (1974). Second language learning—universals? In *Working Papers on Bilingualism* (Vol. 3, pp. 1-18). Toronto: Toronto Institute for Studies in Education.

Heath, S. B. (1983). *Ways with words: Language, life, and work in communities and classrooms.* Cambridge, MA: Cambridge University Press.

Hinton, G. (1989). Learning distributed representations of concepts. In R. G. M. Morris (Ed.), *Parallel distributed processing: Implications for psychology and neurobiology* (pp. 46-61). Oxford: Clarendon.

Hoff-Ginsberg, E. (1991). Mother-child conversation in different social classes and communicative settings. *Child Development, 62,* 782-796.

Honzik, M. P. (1983). Measuring mental abilities in infancy: The value and limitations. In M. Lewis (Ed.), *Origins of intelligence: Infancy and early childhood* (2nd ed., pp. 67-105). New York: Plenum.

Horgan, D. (1980). Nouns: Love 'em or leave 'em. *Annals of the New York Academy of Sciences, 345,* 5-25.

Horgan, D. (1981). Rate of language acquisition and noun emphasis. *Journal of Psycholinguistic Research, 10,* 629-640.

Hudelson, S. (1990). Bilingual/ESL learners talking in the English classroom. In S. Hynds & D. L. Rubin (Eds.), *Perspectives on talk and learning* (pp. 267-283). Urbana, IL: National Council of Teachers of English.

Huxley, R. (1970). The development of the correct use of subject personal pronouns in two children. In G. B. Flores d'Arcais & W. J. M. Levelt (Eds.), *Advances in psycholinguistics* (pp. 141-165). New York: American Elsevier.

Jones, C. P., & Adamson, L. B. (1987). Language use in mother-child and mother-child-sibling interactions. *Child Development, 58,* 356-366.

Kagan, J., Reznick, J. S., Clarke, C., Snidman, N., & Garcia-Coll, C. (1984). Behavioral inhibition to the unfamiliar. *Child Development, 55,* 2212-2225.

Klein, B. V. E. (1978). What is the biology of language? In E. Walker (Ed.), *Explorations in the biology of language* (pp. 1-14). Montgomery, VT: Bradford Books.

Krashen, S., & Scarcella, R. (1978). On routines and patterns in language acquisition and performance. *Language Learning, 28,* 283-300.

Leonard, L. B. (1976). *Meaning in child language.* New York: Grune & Stratton.

Leonard, L., Newhoff, M., & Masalem, L. (1980). Individual differences in early childhood phonology. *Applied Psycholinguistics, 1,* 7-30.

Leonard, L., Schwartz, R., Folger, M., Newhoff, M., & Wilcox, M. (1979). Children's imitations of lexical items. *Child Development, 59,* 19-27.

Lieven, E. M. (1978). Conversations between mothers and young children: Individual differences and their possible implications for the study of language learning. In N. Waterson & C. Snow (Eds.), *The development of communication: Social and pragmatic factors in language acquisition* (pp. 173-187). New York: John Wiley.

Lieven, E., Pine, J., & Barnes, H. (1992). Individual differences in early vocabulary development: Redefining the referential-expressive distinction. *Journal of Child Language, 19,* 287-310.

Locke, J. L. (1988). Variation in human biology and child phonology: A response to Goad and Ingram. *Journal of Child Language, 15,* 663-668.

Lucariello, J., & Nelson, K. (1986). Context effects on lexical specificity in maternal and child discourse. *Journal of Child Language, 13,* 507-522.

Macken, M. (1978). Permitted complexity in phonological development: One child's acquisition of Spanish consonants. *Lingua, 44,* 219-253.

Maratsos, M. (1975). Commentary. *Monographs of the Society for Research in Child Development, 40*(2), 91-94.

Markman, E. M. (1989). *Categorization and naming in children.* Cambridge: MIT Press.

McCall, R. (1981). Nature-nurture and the two realms of development. *Child Development, 52,* 1-12.

McCall, R. B. (1983). A conceptual approach to early mental development. In M. Lewis (Ed.), *Origins of intelligence: Infancy and early childhood* (2nd ed., pp. 107-133). New York: Plenum.

McCall, R., Eichorn, D., & Hogarty, P. (1977). Transitions in early mental development. *Monographs of the Society for Research in Child Development,* Serial No. 171.

McCarthy, D. (1933). Language development. In C. Murchison (Ed.), *A handbook of child psychology* (pp. 278-315). Worcester, MA: Clark University Press.

McClelland, J. L. (1989). Parallel distributed processing: Implications for cognition and development. In R. G. M. Morris (Ed.), *Parallel distributed processing: Implications for psychology and neurobiology* (pp. 8-45). Oxford: Clarendon.

Munsinger, H., & Douglass, A. I. I. (1976). The syntactic abilities of identical twins, fraternal twins, and their siblings. *Child Development, 47,* 40-50.

Nelson, K. (1973). Structure and strategy in learning to talk. *Monographs of the Society for Research in Child Development, 38*(1-2, Serial No. 149).

Nelson, K. (1975). The nominal shift in semantic-syntactic development. *Cognitive Psychology, 7,* 461-479.

Nelson, K. (1981). Individual differences in language development: Implications for development and language. *Developmental Psychology, 17,* 170-187.

Nelson, K. (1985). *Making sense: The acquisition of shared meaning.* San Diego: Academic Press.

Nelson, K., Hampson, J., & Shaw, L. K. (1993). Nouns in early lexicons: Evidence, explanations and implications. *Journal of Child Language, 20,* 61-84.

Nelson, K. E., Baker, N., Denniger, M., Bonvillian, J., & Kaplan, B. (1985). "Cookie" versus "Do-it-again": Imitative-referential and personal-social syntactic-initiating styles in young children. *Linguistics, 23,* 433-454.

Oyama, S. (1985). *The ontogeny of information.* Cambridge, MA: Cambridge University Press.

Peters, A. M. (1977). Language learning strategies: Does the whole equal the sum of the parts? *Language, 53,* 560-573.

Peters, A. M. (1983). *The units of language acquisition.* Cambridge, UK: Cambridge University Press.

Pine, J. (1992). Functional basis of referentiality. *First Language, 12*(34), 39-55.

Pine, J. M., & Lieven, E. V. M. (1990). Referential style at thirteen months: Why age-defined cross-sectional measures are inappropriate for the study of strategy differences in early language development. *Journal of Child Language, 17,* 625-631.

Pinker, S. (1984). *Language learnability and language development.* Cambridge, MA: Harvard University Press.

Plunkett, K. (1985). Learning strategies in two Danish children's language development. *Papers and Reports on Child Language Development, 24,* 105-114.

Plunkett, K. (1993). Lexical segmentation and vocabulary growth in early language acquisition. *Journal of Child Language, 20,* 43-60.

Plunkett, K., & Sinha, C. (1992). Connectionism and developmental theory. *British Journal of Developmental Psychology, 10,* 209-254.

Ramer, A. (1976). Syntactic styles in emerging language. *Journal of Child Language,* *3,* 49-62.

Rescorla, L. A. (1984). Individual differences in early language development and their predictive significance. *Acta Paedologica, 1,* 97-116.

Richards, B. J. (1990). *Language development and individual differences: A study of auxiliary verb learning.* Cambridge, UK: Cambridge University Press.

Rosenblatt, D. (1977). Developmental trends in infant play. In B. Tizard & D. Harvey (Eds.), *Biology of play* (pp. 33-44). London: William Heinemann Medical Books.

Salkin, S. (1985). *Relationships between mothers' speech and children's language style.* Unpublished senior honors thesis, Miami University, Oxford, OH.

Shaffer, D. R. (1993). *Developmental psychology: Childhood and adolescence* (3rd ed.). Belmont, CA: Brooks/Cole.

Shore, C. (1986). Combinatorial play, conceptual development and early multi-word speech. *Developmental Psychology, 22,* 184-190.

Shore, C., Bates, E., Bretherton, I., Beeghly, M., & O'Connell, B. (1990). Vocal and gestural symbols: Similarities and differences from 13 to 28 months. In V. Volterra & C. J. Erting (Eds.), *From gesture to language in hearing and deaf children* (pp. 79-92). New York: Springer-Verlag.

Shore, C., & Bauer, P. (1983, August). *Individual styles in language and symbolic play.* Paper presented at the annual meeting of the American Psychological Association, Anaheim, CA.

Shore, C., & Bauer, P. (April, 1984). *Language styles and symbolic play.* Paper presented at the International Conference on Infant Studies, New York, NY.

Shore, C., Dixon, W. E., Jr., & Bauer, P. (in press). Measures of linguistic and non-linguistic knowledge of objects in the second year. *First Language.*

Shore, C., Dixon, W. E., Jr., Geiger, S., Gittings, A., Bodle, J., & Zhou, L. (1992, May). *Effects of time and situation on parental speech to infants.* Paper presented at the International Conference on Infant Studies, Miami Beach, FL.

Shotwell, J. M., Wolf, D., & Gardner, H. (1979). Exploring early symbolization: Styles of achievement. In B. Sutton-Smith (Ed.), *Play and learning* (pp. 127-156). New York: Gardner.

Slobin, D. I. (1982). Universal and particular in the acquisition of language. In L. R. Gleitman & E. Wanner (Eds.), *Language acquisition: The state of the art* (pp. 128-170). Cambridge, UK: Cambridge University Press.

Slomkowski, C. L., Nelson, K., Dunn, J., & Plomin, R. (1992). Temperament and language: Relations from toddlerhood to middle childhood. *Developmental Psychology, 28,* 1090-1095.

Snyder, L., Bates, E., & Bretherton, I. (1981). Content and context in early lexical development. *Journal of Child Language, 8,* 565-582.

Starr, S. (1975). The relationship of single words to two-word sentences. *Child Development, 46,* 701-708.

Stoel-Gammon, C., & Cooper, J. A. (1984). Patterns of early lexical and phonological development. *Journal of Child Language, 11,* 247-271.

Thal, D. J., Marchman, V., Stiles, J., Aram, D., Trauner, D., Nass, R., & Bates, E. (1991). Early lexical development in children with focal brain injury. *Brain and Language, 40,* 491-527.

Thelen, E. (1990). Dynamical systems and the generation of individual differences. In J. Colombo & J. Fagen (Eds.), *Individual differences in infancy: Reliability, stability, prediction* (pp. 19-44). Hillsdale, NJ: Lawrence Erlbaum.

Thelen, E. (1992). Development as a dynamic system. *Current Directions in Psycho logical Science, 1,* 189-193.

Thompson, L. A., & Plomin, R. (1988). The Sequenced Inventory of Communication Development: An adoption study of two- and three-year-olds. *International Journal of Behavioral Development, 11,* 219-231.

Tomasello, M., & Todd, J. (1983). Joint attention and lexical acquisition styles. *First Language, 4,* 197-212.

Vihman, M. (1981). Phonology and the development of the lexicon: Evidence from children's errors. *Journal of Child Language, 8,* 239-264.

Vihman, M. M. (1986). Individual differences in babbling and early speech: Predicting to age three. In B. Lindblom & R. Zetterstrom (Eds.), *Precursors of early speech* (Wenner-Gren International Symposium Series, Vol. 44, pp. 95-107). New York: Stockton Press.

Vihman, M. M., Ferguson, C. A., & Elbert, M. (1986). Phonological development from babbling to speech: Common tendencies and individual differences. *Applied Psycholinguistics, 7,* 3-40.

Vihman, M. M., & Greenlee, M. (1987). Individual differences in phonological development: Ages 1 and 3 years. *Journal of Speech and Hearing Research, 30,* 503-521.

Wachs, T. D. (1993). Multidimensional correlates of individual variability in play and exploration. In M. H. Bornstein & A. W. O'Reilly (Eds.), *The role of play in the development of thought* (New Directions for Child Development, Vol. 59, pp. 43-53). San Francisco: Jossey-Bass.

Werner, H., & Kaplan, B. (1963). *Symbol formation: An organismic-developmental approach to language and the expression of thought.* New York: John Wiley.

Wertsch, J. V., & Stone, C. A. (1985). The concept of internalization of Vygotsky's account of the genesis of higher mental functions. In J. V. Wertsch (Ed.), *Culture, communication and cognition: Vygotskian perspectives* (pp. 162-179). Cambridge, MA: Cambridge University Press.

Wiley, A., Shore, C., & Dixon, W. E., Jr. (1989, April). *Situational differences in the type of utterances mothers use with thirteen-month-old children.* Paper presented at the biennial meeting of the Society for Research in Child Development, Kansas City, MO.

Wolf, D., & Gardner, H. (1979). Style and sequence in symbolic play. In M. Franklin & N. Smith (Eds.), *Early symbolization* (pp. 117-138). Hillsdale, NJ: Lawrence Erlbaum.

Wolf, D., & Grollman, S. H. (1982). Ways of playing: Individual differences in imaginative style. In D. J. Pepler & K. H. Rubin (Eds.), *The play of children: Current theory and research* (pp. 46-63). Basel, Switzerland: Karger.

Zaidel, E. (1983). A response to Gazzaniga: Language in the right hemisphere. *American Psychologist, 38,* 542-546.

Name Index

Subject Index

Analytic versus holistic, 51, 68, 69, 109
  and cognitive development, 87-88
  and comprehension, 107
  and content words, 55
  and explanations of grammatical
    development, 33, 105, 125
  and function words, 30-31, 55
  and language disorders, 111
  and language functions, 40-42, 51,
    80-82, 125
  and phonological development, 33-
    36
  and symbolic play, 86-87
  as multiple dimensioyns, 125
  as "stable attractors," 115
  continuity from 13 to 28 months, 54-
    56
  defined, 15, 22-23, 25
  information processing, 88
  utility of, 32-33
  See also Cognitive components; For-
    mulaic utterances
Articulation. See Intelligibility
Attention, 91-93, 101, 106, 108
Autonomous subsystems of language:
  and language styles, 95-96, 100,
    102
  behavior genetics, 72, 79, 108

See Biological bases; Domain specificity; Environment; Phonological develoment; Syntax

Behaviorism. See Empiricism
Biological bases of language:
  and language styles 95-101, 106
  See also Behavior genetics; Environ-
    ment; Modularity; Nativism
Bidirectionality of influence, 72, 78,
  100, 102, 113
  See also Social support for language
Birth order, 73-74, 103
Bold versus timid. See Risk taking ver-
  sus conservative; Temperament
Bootstrapping hypothesis, 21

Cases (e.g., agent, patient).
  See Nominal versus pronominal,
    relation to meaning categories
Categorization, 20, 43-44
Chaos theory. See Nonlinear dynamic
  systems theory
Closed-class words. See Function words
Cognitive components of language, 6,
  7, 11

About the Author

Cecilia Shore is Associate Professor of Psychology at Miami University in Oxford, Ohio. She received her B.A. in 1977 from the University of Kansas and her Ph.D. from the University of Colorado at Boulder in 1981. Her research involves cognitive and language development in infants and toddlers, specifically relationships between language and play. Her recent research has focused on individual differences in language and situational effects on what parents say to children. Her other research interests include the relations between conceptual and semantic development and memory for causal events.